CONTENTS

Chapter One: Eating Disorders

Chapter Two: Obesity

Introduction

Eating Disorders is the one hundred and twenty-seventh volume in the **Issues** series. The aim of this series is to offer up-to-date information about important issues in our world.

Eating Disorders looks at eating disorders such as anorexia nervosa, bulimia nervosa and binge eating disorder, as well as the growing problem of obesity in the UK.

The information comes from a wide variety of sources and includes:
Government reports and statistics
Newspaper reports and features
Magazine articles and surveys
Website material
Literature from lobby groups
and charitable organisations.

It is hoped that, as you read about the many aspects of the issues explored in this book, you will critically evaluate the information presented. It is important that you decide whether you are being presented with facts or opinions. Does the writer give a biased or an unbiased report? If an opinion is being expressed, do you agree with the writer?

Eating Disorders offers a useful starting-point for those who need convenient access to information about the many issues involved. However, it is only a starting-point. Following each article is a URL to the relevant organisation's website, which you may wish to visit for further information.

*****

Eating Disorders

12

Series Editor

Craig Donnellan

Assistant Editor

Lisa Firth

Independence

Educational Publishers
Cambridge

First published by Independence
PO Box 295
Cambridge CB1 3XP
England

British Library Cataloguing in Publication Data
Eating Disorders – (Issues Series)
I. Donnellan, Craig II. Series
616.8'526

ISBN 1 86168 366 9

Printed in Great Britain
MWL Print Group Ltd

Layout by
Lisa Firth

Cover
The illustration on the front cover is by
Simon Kneebone.

Eating disorders

Information from the Royal College of Psychiatrists

Introduction

We all have different eating habits. There are a large number of 'eating styles' which can allow us to stay healthy. However, there are some which are driven by an intense fear of becoming fat and which actually damage our health. These are called 'eating disorders' and involve:

- eating too much;
- eating too little;
- using harmful ways to get rid of calories.

This article deals with two eating disorders – anorexia nervosa and bulimia nervosa. It describes the two disorders separately:

- the symptoms of anorexia and bulimia are often mixed – some people say that they have 'bulimarexia';
- the pattern of symptoms can change over time – you may start with anorexic symptoms, but later develop the symptoms of bulimia.

Who gets eating disorders?

Girls and women are 10 times more likely than boys and men to suffer from anorexia or bulimia. However, eating disorders do seem to be getting more common in boys and men. They occur more often in people who have been overweight as children.

Anorexia nervosa

What are the signs?
You find that you:

- worry more and more about your weight;
- eat less and less;
- exercise more and more, to burn off calories;
- can't stop losing weight, even when you are well below a safe weight for your age and height;
- smoke more or chew gum to keep your weight down;
- lose interest in sex.

In girls or women – monthly menstrual periods become irregular or stop.

In men or boys – erections and wet dreams stop, testicles shrink.

When does it start?
Usually in the teenage years. It affects around:

- one 15-year-old girl in every 150;
- one 15-year-old boy in every 1,000.

It can also start in childhood or in later life.

What happens?

- You take in very few calories every day. You eat 'healthily' – fruit, vegetables and salads – but they don't give your body enough energy.
- You may also exercise, use slimming pills, or smoke more to keep your weight down.
- You don't want to eat yourself, but you buy food and cook for other people.
- You still get as hungry as ever, in fact you can't stop thinking about food.
- You become more afraid of putting on weight, and more determined to keep your weight well below normal.
- Your family may be the first to notice your thinness and weight loss.

- You may find yourself lying to other people about the amount you are eating and how much weight you are losing.
- You may also develop some of the symptoms of bulimia. Unlike someone with bulimia nervosa, your weight may continue to be very low.

Bulimia nervosa

What are the signs?
You find that you:

- worry more and more about your weight;
- binge eat;
- make yourself vomit and/or use laxatives to get rid of calories;
- have irregular menstrual periods;
- feel tired;
- feel guilty;
- stay a normal weight, in spite of your efforts to diet.

When does it start?
Bulimia nervosa often starts in the mid-teens. However, people don't usually seek help for it until their early to mid-twenties because they are able to hide it, even though it affects their work and social life. People most often seek help when their life changes – the start of a new relationship or having to live with other people for the first time.

About four out of every 100 women suffers from bulimia at some time in their lives; rather fewer men.

Bingeing

You raid the fridge or go out and buy lots of fattening foods that you would normally avoid. You then go back to your room, or home, and eat it all, quickly, in secret. You might get through packets of biscuits, several boxes of chocolates and a number of cakes in just a couple of hours. You may even take someone else's food, or shoplift, to satisfy the urge to binge.

Afterwards you feel stuffed and bloated – and probably guilty and depressed. You try to get rid of the food you have eaten by making yourself sick, or by purging with laxatives. It is very uncomfortable and tiring, but you find yourself trapped in a routine of binge eating, and vomiting and/or purging.

Binge eating disorder

This is a pattern of behaviour that has recently been recognised. It involves dieting and binge eating, but not vomiting. It is distressing, but much less harmful than bulimia. Sufferers are more likely to become overweight.

How can anorexia and bulimia affect you?

If you aren't getting enough calories, you may experience the following.

Psychological symptoms
- Sleep badly.
- Find it difficult to concentrate or think clearly about anything other than food or calories.
- Feel depressed.
- Lose interest in other people.
- Become obsessive about food and eating (and sometimes other things such as washing, cleaning or tidiness).

Physical symptoms
- Find it harder to eat because your stomach has shrunk.
- Feel tired, weak and cold as your body's metabolism slows down.
- Become constipated.
- Not grow to your full height.
- Get brittle bones which break easily.
- Be unable to get pregnant.
- Damage your liver, particularly if you drink alcohol.
- In extreme cases, you may die. Anorexia nervosa has the highest death rate of any psychological disorder.

If you vomit, you may:
- lose the enamel on your teeth (it is dissolved by the stomach acid in your vomit);
- get a puffy face (the salivary glands in your cheeks swell up);
- notice your heart beating irregularly – palpitations (vomiting disturbs the balance of salts in your blood);
- feel weak;
- feel tired all the time;
- damage your kidneys;
- have epileptic fits;
- be unable to get pregnant.

If you use laxatives regularly, you may:
- have persistent stomach pain;
- get swollen fingers;
- find that you can't go to the toilet any more without using laxatives (using laxatives all the time can damage the muscles in your bowel);
- have huge weight swings. You lose lots of fluid when you purge, but take it all in again when you drink water afterwards (no calories are lost using laxatives).

What causes eating disorders?

There is no simple answer, but these ideas have all been suggested as explanations.

Social pressure
Our social surroundings powerfully influence our behaviour. Societies which don't value thinness have fewer eating disorders. Places where thinness is valued, such as ballet schools, have more eating disorders. 'Thin is beautiful' in western culture. Television, newspapers and magazines show pictures of idealised, artificially slim people. So, at some time or other, most of us try to diet. Some of us diet too much, and slip into anorexia.

Lack of an 'off' switch
Most of us can only diet so much before our body tells us that it is time to start eating again. Some people with anorexia may not have this same body 'switch' and can keep their body weight dangerously low for a long time.

Control
It can be very satisfying to diet. Most of us know the feeling of achievement when the scales tell us that we have lost a couple of pounds. It is good to feel that we can control ourselves in a clear, visible way. It may be that your weight is the only part of your life over which you feel you do have any control.

Puberty
Anorexia can reverse some of the physical changes of becoming an adult – pubic and facial hair in men, breasts and menstrual periods in women. This may help to put off the demands of getting older, particularly sexual ones.

Family
Eating is an important part of our lives with other people. Accepting food gives pleasure and refusing it will often upset someone. This is particularly true within families. Saying 'no' to food may be the only way you can express your feelings, or have any say in family affairs.

Depression
Most of us have eaten for comfort when we have been upset, or even just bored. People with bulimia are often depressed, and it may be that binges start off as a way of coping with feelings of unhappiness. Unfortunately, vomiting and using laxatives can leave you feeling just as bad.

Low self-esteem
People with anorexia and bulimia often don't think much of themselves, and compare themselves unfavourably to other people. Losing weight can be a way of trying to get a sense of respect and self-worth.

Emotional distress

We all react differently when bad things happen, or when our lives change. Anorexia and bulimia have been related to:

- life difficulties;
- sexual abuse;
- physical illness;
- upsetting events – a death or the break-up of a relationship;
- important events – marriage or leaving home.

The vicious circle

An eating disorder can continue even when the original stress or reason for it has passed. Once your stomach has shrunk, it can feel uncomfortable and frightening to eat.

Physical causes

Some doctors think that there may be a physical cause that we don't yet understand.

Is it different for men?

- Eating disorders do seem to have become more common in boys and men.
- Eating disorders are more common in occupations which demand a low body weight (or low body fat). These include body building, wrestling, dancing, swimming, and athletics.
- It may be that men are now seeking help for eating disorders rather than keeping quiet about them.

People with special needs and younger children

A learning difficulty, autism or some other developmental problems can disrupt eating. For example, some people with autism may take a dislike to the colour or texture of foods, and refuse to eat them. The eating problems of pre-teen children are more to do with food texture, 'picky eating' or being angry rather than with wanting to be very thin. The ways of helping these problems are rather different from those for anorexia and bulimia.

Do I have a problem?

A questionnaire used by doctors asks:

- do you make yourself sick because you're uncomfortably full?

- do you worry that you've lost control over how much you eat?
- have you recently lost more than 6 kilograms (about a stone) in three months?
- do you believe you're fat when others say you're thin?
- would you say that food dominates your life?

If you answer 'yes' to two or more of these questions, you may have a problem with your eating.

Helping yourself

- Bulimia can sometimes be tackled using a self-help manual with some guidance from a therapist.
- Anorexia usually needs more organised help from a clinic or therapist. It is still worth getting as much information as you can about the options, so that you can make the best choices for yourself.

Things to do

- Stick to regular mealtimes – breakfast, lunch and dinner. If your weight is very low, have morning, afternoon and night-time snacks.
- Try to think of one small step you could take towards a healthier way of eating. If you can't face eating breakfast, try sitting at the table for a few minutes at breakfast time and just drinking a glass of water. When you have got used to doing this, have just a little to eat, even half a slice of toast – but do it every day.
- Keep a diary of what you eat, when you eat it and what your thoughts and feelings have been every day. You can use this to see if there are connections between how you feel, what you are thinking about, and how you eat.
- Try to be honest about what you are or are not eating, both with yourself and with other people.
- Remind yourself that you don't always have to be achieving things – let yourself off the hook sometimes.
- Remind yourself that, if you lose more weight, you will feel more anxious and depressed.
- Make two lists – one of what your eating disorder has given you, one of what you have lost through it.

A self-help book can help you with this.

- Try to be kind to your body, don't punish it.
- Make sure you know what a reasonable weight is for you, and that you understand why.
- Read stories of other people's experiences of recovery. You can find these in self-help books or on the Internet.
- Think about joining a self-help group. Your GP may be able to recommend one, or you can contact the Eating Disorders Association.

Things not to do

- Don't weigh yourself more than once a week.
- Don't spend time checking your body and looking at yourself in the mirror. Nobody is perfect. The longer you look at yourself, the more likely you are to find something you don't like. Constant checking can make the most attractive person unhappy with the way they look.
- Don't cut yourself off from family and friends. You may want to because they think you are too thin, but they can be a lifeline.
- Avoid websites that encourage you to lose weight and stay at a very low body weight. They encourage you to damage your health, but won't do anything to help when you fall ill.

What if I don't have any help or don't change my eating habits?

Most people with a serious eating disorder will end up having some sort of treatment, so it is not clear what will happen if nothing is done. However, it looks as though most serious eating disorders don't get better on their own. Some sufferers from anorexia will die – this is less likely to happen if you do not vomit, do not use laxatives and do not drink alcohol.

- The above information is an extract from the Royal College of Psychiatrists' leaflet 'Eating Disorders' and is reprinted with permission. Visit www.rcpsych.ac.uk for more information.

© Royal College of Psychiatrists

Eating disorders: the risks

Anorexia nervosa, bulimia nervosa, and compulsive eating carry many risks, and can even be fatal

Short term

People with eating disorders start to withdraw from normal friends and activities as they become more obsessive, miserable or ashamed. Bulimics are most at risk of developing a pattern of drug or alcohol abuse. In rare cases, bulimics can cause severe damage to their bodies by making themselves vomit. Hard retching can tear the oesophagus, and prolonged vomiting sometimes causes dangerous imbalances in the electrolytes (minerals and ions) in body fluids.

People with eating disorders start to withdraw from normal friends and activities as they become more obsessive, miserable or ashamed

Medium term

Anorexics who continue to starve themselves cause chemical and hormonal changes in their bodies that lead to loss of appetite, periods stopping, and feelings of depression and sadness. The gut is also affected, increasing the chances of constipation. Continued abuse of laxatives can permanently affect the way the bowels work, and abuse of slimming pills has the same risks as amphetamine abuse. The longer the eating disorder goes on, the harder it is to treat. Bulimics start to erode their tooth enamel because of the acid damage caused by being sick. They can also find that their periods become irregular or stop.

Long term

If eating disorders are left untreated for a long time, serious complications and even death can follow. The effects of anorexic starvation become more severe, and the lack of nutrients takes its toll. Shortages of iron and calcium cause anaemia and osteoporosis (brittle bones). Lack of protein affects the heart muscle, causing irregularities. There is a greater chance of hypothermia because there is not enough energy to keep warm, and fine wispy body hair called laguno starts to grow. Bulimics can get stomach problems including ulcers, anaemia, and swollen saliva glands that can result in puffed-up cheeks. Compulsive overeaters are at risk of developing health problems associated with obesity, including high blood pressure, heart disease, and damage to joints.

■ The above information is reprinted with kind permission from TheSite.org. Visit www.thesite.org for more information.

© TheSite.org

Symptoms of an eating disorder

Physical signs	Behavioural signs	Psychological signs
Anorexia Nervosa	**Anorexia Nervosa**	**Anorexia Nervosa**
Severe weight loss Periods stopping Hormonal changes in men and boys Difficulty sleeping Dizziness Stomach pains Constipation Poor circulation and feeling cold	Wanting to be left alone Wearing big baggy clothes Excessive exercising Lying about eating meals Denying there is a problem Difficulty concentrating Wanting to have control	Intense fear of gaining weight Depressed Feeling emotional Obsession with dieting Mood swings Distorted perception of body weight and size
Bulimia Nervosa	**Bulimia Nervosa**	**Bulimia Nervosa**
Sore throat/swollen glands Stomach pains Mouth infections Irregular periods Dry or poor skin Difficulty sleeping Sensitive or damaged teeth	Eating large quantities of food Being sick after eating Being secretive	Feeling ashamed, depressed and guilty Feeling out of control Mood swings
Binge Eating	**Binge Eating**	**Binge Eating**
Weight gain	Eating large quantities of food Eating inappropriate food Being secretive	Feeling depressed and out of control Mood swings Emotional behaviour

Source: Eating Disorders Association (www.edauk.com)

Can eating disorders cause permanent damage?

Information from the Institute of Psychiatry, King's College London

It is difficult to answer this with confidence, as there have been relatively few studies which have followed the health of sufferers over time.

Most of the physical problems do reverse with weight gain, or if the weight control practices stop. It may depend on the duration of the illness and the stage of life at which the illness arose. For example, there may be a critical time at which puberty can take place.

If the illness strikes before all stages of puberty have been attained and recovery is delayed, there may be irreversible failure to achieve growth in stature, peak bone density and secondary sexual development.

Adolescence is also a critical period for cognitive and psychosocial development, and it is simply not known whether an individual will be able to reach their full potential in cognitive and psychosocial development if they recover after this critical period has passed.

The reproductive system

It is probable that, if there is full recovery, then all will return to normal, although it may take longer than normal to conceive. In some cases, it may be necessary to have hormonal treatment. The difficulty is that between one-third and one-half of all sufferers may have residual problems and are still under their optimal weight.

Bone density

We do not know by how much bone density recovers. There is some evidence that with a short illness the bones can regain their strength and thickness. It may take a long time for the repairs to be completed and some sites are repaired before others. Recovery may be incomplete. If the bones remain thin, the risk of fracture is increased. Bones in the spinal column may be crushed, and the spinal curvature and subsequent loss of height are irreversible. This may lead to chronic pain.

Heart and circulation

In the general population 'yo-yo' dieting is associated with an increased risk of cardiovascular disease and death. Patients on very low fat diets often have raised levels of cholesterol, which may be a risk factor for heart disease.

> *Whatever the long-term damage to physical health, the one thing that can never be recovered is lost time*

Intestinal problems

After recovery these may remain. Heartburn and stomach ulcers are more common. The bowel can become 'irritable', with frequent diarrhoea or severe constipation.

Kidneys

Weight control measures that alter salt and water balance can lead to permanent kidney damage. As the kidneys have a lot of reserve function this may not become apparent unless they are put under further stress.

Time and lost opportunities

Whatever the long-term damage to physical health, the one thing that can never be recovered is lost time. Individuals who overcome eating disorders after a number of years often express great sadness for all the missed opportunities, as illustrated by these quotations:

'Recovery for me involved grieving for past pain and for time spent not allowing myself to be happy.'

'I find myself yearning for the teenage years I missed out on completely. Sometimes the pain is so great, it stops me enjoying to the full the good things I have gained since recovery. And then I realise what I am doing, and force myself to return to the present before I lose any more time!'

■ The above information is reprinted with kind permission from the Institute of Psychiatry, King's College London. Visit www.iop.kcl.ac.uk for more information.

© Institute of Psychiatry, King's College London

Genetics and biology

While genetic and biological predispositions in anorexia, bulimia and compulsive overeating are important to explore, for each individual there may be a wide variety of reasons for developing an eating disorder

A great deal of research in recent years has indicated that there may be genetic factors that contribute to the onset of an eating disorder. This is not to say that emotional, behavioural and environmental reasons do not play significant roles, but that for some, there may be a genetic predisposition to the development of anorexia, bulimia or compulsive overeating.

One study by doctors at the Maudsley Hospital in London suggested that people with anorexia were twice as likely to have variations in the gene for serotonin receptors, part of which helps to determine appetite. Because of an overproduction of serotonin, it is possible that those with anorexia are in a continual state of feeling acute stress – as in the fight or flight response – creating an overwhelming and constant sense of anxiety.

Another study, by Dr Walter Kaye of the University of Pittsburgh, examined a number of recovered bulimia patients. They were monitored for persistent behaviour disturbances and levels of serotonin, dopamine and norepinephrine. His team found that, compared to people with no history of bulimia, the recovered individuals still had abnormal serotonin levels, with overall more negative moods, and obsessions with perfectionism and exactness. The levels of the other brain chemicals, dopamine and norepinephrine, were normal in comparison.

What is serotonin?

Serotonin (ser-oh-TOH-nin) is a neurotransmitter, a group of chemical messengers, that carry out communication in the brain and body. The messengers travel from one neuron (or nerve cell) to others that act as receivers, where they attach to

a specific area called a receptor site. This union, like a key fitting into a lock, triggers signals that either allow or prevent a message to be passed on to other cells. Since the discovery of serotonin in the 1950s, researchers are finding evidence that one of its roles is to mediate emotions and judgement (*Serotonin and Judgement*; Society for Neuroscience).

A great deal of research in recent years has indicated that there may be genetic factors that contribute to the onset of an eating disorder

---

Serotonin is involved in many behaviours such as hunger, sleep, sexual response, impulse control, aggressive behaviour and anger, depression, anxiety and perception. Abnormally low levels of serotonin might be found in someone who is suicidal, who is particularly agressive towards others, or a person who is extremely depressed. High levels of serotonin may be found in a person who is in a constant state of anxiety, has a tendency to be over-exacting in completing tasks, who suffers insomnia, or who has a tendency to feel overly-stimulated by their surroundings (overwhelmed).

So how might this translate for someone with an eating disorder?

Low levels of serotonin, which could contribute to a person's sense of depression, are in theory increased during episodes of bingeing, making the person actually feel better. As theorised, bingeing on sweets, starches or carbohydrates would increase serotonin and produce a sense of well-being.

The exact opposite would be true in conjunction with self-starvation or restriction. If too much serotonin is present, this may create a sense of perpetual anxiety, and in theory, by reducing the intake of calories to starvation level, the result would be a calming effect or sense of regaining control.

In other words, those with low or high levels of serotonin may feel 'driven' towards eating or not eating as they consciously or subconsciously realise it actually makes them feel better emotionally, because of a physical response in their brain.

It is very important to note that the act of restricting, and bingeing (with or without purging) can also lead to a disruption in serotonin levels, thus contributing to an already existing problem, or creating a completely new one to deal with. This can lead to depression and anxiety, which are known side-effects of malnutrition and vitamin deficiencies, both for undereaters and overeaters.

In addition to depression and anxiety, abnormal serotonin levels have been found in people with other mental illness, such as obsessive compulsive disorder, bipolar disorder, borderline personality disorder, and attention-deficit/hyperactivity disorder (ADHD), all of which can, for some, co-exist with an eating disorder. Studies also suggest that there are genetic predispositions to serotonin disruptions that appear to run in some families.

Not the only factor

While all of the genetic studies and biological predispositions may be important to understand, it is essential to realise that there are people who live with too much or too little serotonin who do not develop an eating disorder. It is also important to note that there are people who develop an eating disorder who have no corresponding predisposition. While there may be genes that play a role in the level of serotonin within our brains (for some people), the emphasis on emotional, behavioural and environmental factors cannot and should not be dismissed. For some, low or high levels of serotonin may make a person predisposed to relying on food as a way to control how they feel, but that doesn't eliminate all of the non-biological possibilities.

One study suggested that people with anorexia were twice as likely to have variations in the gene for serotonin receptors, part of which helps to determine appetite

---

One way to look at this is to examine a child with attention deficit disorder (ADD), that has a parent with ADD. The family environment may be very chaotic, in part due to the way they are hard-wired, but also because of an inability to cope effectively with the ADD. These behavioural patterns, as well as a sense of instability in the environement, are as much a contribution to the way the child learns to cope, as is the genetic influence of ADD. One doctor we spoke with said, 'I find that a really high percentage of the [eating disorders] clients I work with have parents with some kind of undiagnosed anxiety or compulsive

behaviour type. They may learn how to have these behaviours themselves simply by living in such an environment. Only when they grow up and leave the home do they even have the opportunity to see that what they learned may be dysfunctional.'

As stressed above, there are many things that may play a role in the onset of an eating disorder; family environments, the way a person was taught to (and how they) cope with their emotions, how they were taught to (and how they) communicate, their general sense of self-esteem, and possible issues of physical, emotional or sexual abuse. Another factor may be a history of addiction to drugs or alcohol in a family, and the effect it may play both genetically and environmentally. The problems each person faces, the way they cope, the reasons for continuing to hurt or punish themselves, and the way they feel are all critical issues that cannot be tossed aside.

Keep in mind, low levels of serotonin have been discovered in some alcoholics as well, but not everyone with a low level of serotonin would become an alcoholic, stressing the point that there are other contributing factors.

Though serotonin may play a role in feeling depressed or overly anxious, it is *not* the only reason people suffer from depression or anxiety, nor the only reason they may develop an eating disorder. It may, for some, be an important piece to the puzzle, but isn't by itself a complete picture.

'Although no one can yet say for certain, new science is offering tantalising clues. Doctors now compare anorexia to alcoholism and depression, potentially fatal diseases that may be set off by environmental factors such as stress or trauma, but have their roots in a complex combination of genes and brain chemistry. In other words, many kids are affected by pressure-cooker school environments and a culture of thinness promoted by magazines and music videos, but most of them don't secretly scrape their dinner into the garbage. The environment "pulls the trigger",' says Cynthia Bulik, Director of the Eating Disorder Program at

the University of North Carolina at Chapel Hill. 'But it's a child's latent vulnerabilities that "load the gun".' (*Newsweek*, December 2005, 'Fighting Anorexia: No One to Blame')

What do we do with this information?

Keeping the big picture in mind, it may be useful to be aware of how serotonin levels affect each particular person when it comes to their course of treatment. Medications such as SSRIs (selective serotonin re-uptake inhibitors) can help to control levels of serotonin and assist patients in responding more positively to therapy and treatment... but there is no 'magic pill'. Each individual will ultimately respond best when they can find a therapist and treatment team that can address all issues.

Each eating disorder sufferer is an individual. Some may respond to medication, some may not, and some may not wish to take it at all. Some may endure 'the serotonin roller-coaster ride' while trying to find the healthy middle-ground in which the medication becomes effective. It is important for those in recovery, along with their doctors and therapists, to keep all of this in mind, communicate about what is going on, and to remain patient through the process.

■ The above information is reprinted with kind permission from Something Fishy. Visit www.something-fishy.org for more information.

© *Something Fishy*

Are you at risk?
Take a self-test

The following questionnaire can help you decide if you have an eating disorder, or if you are at risk of developing one

☐ *True* ☐ *False*
Even though people tell me I'm thin, I feel fat.

☐ *True* ☐ *False*
I get anxious if I can't exercise.

☐ *True* ☐ *False*
[Female] My menstrual periods are irregular or absent.
[Male] My sex drive is not as strong as it used to be.

☐ *True* ☐ *False*
I worry about what I will eat.

☐ *True* ☐ *False*
If I gain weight, I get anxious and depressed.

☐ *True* ☐ *False*
I would rather eat by myself than with family or friends.

☐ *True* ☐ *False*
Other people talk about the way I eat.

☐ *True* ☐ *False*
I get anxious when people urge me to eat.

☐ *True* ☐ *False*
I don't talk much about my fear of being fat because no one understands how I feel.

☐ *True* ☐ *False*
I enjoy cooking for others, but I usually don't eat what I've cooked.

☐ *True* ☐ *False*
I have a secret stash of food.

☐ *True* ☐ *False*
When I eat, I'm afraid I won't be able to stop.

☐ *True* ☐ *False*
I lie about what I eat.

☐ *True* ☐ *False*
I don't like to be bothered or interrupted when I'm eating.

☐ *True* ☐ *False*
If I were thinner, I would like myself better.

ANRED
Anorexia Nervosa and Related Eating Disorders, Inc.

☐ *True* ☐ *False*
I like to read recipes, cookbooks, calorie charts, and books about dieting and exercise.

☐ *True* ☐ *False*
I have missed work or school because of my weight or eating habits.

☐ *True* ☐ *False*
I tend to be depressed and irritable.

☐ *True* ☐ *False*
I feel guilty when I eat.

☐ *True* ☐ *False*
I avoid some people because they bug me about the way I eat.

☐ *True* ☐ *False*
When I eat, I feel bloated and fat.

☐ *True* ☐ *False*
My eating habits and fear of food interfere with friendships or romantic relationships.

☐ *True* ☐ *False*
I binge eat.

☐ *True* ☐ *False*
I do strange things with my food (cut it into tiny pieces, eat it in special ways, eat it on special dishes with special utensils, make patterns on my plate with it, secretly throw it away, give it to the dog, hide it, spit it out before I swallow, etc.)

☐ *True* ☐ *False*
I get anxious when people watch me eat.

☐ *True* ☐ *False*
I am hardly ever satisfied with myself.

☐ *True* ☐ *False*
I vomit or take laxatives to control my weight.

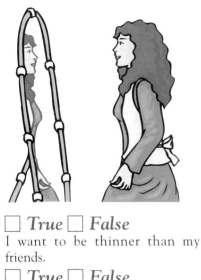

☐ *True* ☐ *False*
I want to be thinner than my friends.

☐ *True* ☐ *False*
I have said or thought, 'I would rather die than be fat.'

☐ *True* ☐ *False*
I have stolen food, laxatives, or diet pills from stores or from other people.

☐ *True* ☐ *False*
I have fasted to lose weight.

☐ *True* ☐ *False*
In romantic moments, I cannot let myself go because I am worried about my fat and flab.

☐ *True* ☐ *False*
I have noticed one or more of the following: cold hands and feet, dry skin, thinning hair, fragile nails, swollen glands in my neck, dental cavities, dizziness, weakness, fainting, rapid or irregular heartbeat.

Discussion and scoring

As strange as it seems in our thin-obsessed society, none of the above behaviours is normal or healthy. Because of unhealthy demands for unrealistic thinness, most women – and a lot of men – will check a few of the above items 'True'. But remember, the more items you have marked 'True', the more serious your situation may be. Please consult with your physician or a qualified mental health counsellor to prevent medical and psychological problems. You could show the person this questionnaire and the items you have circled as a way to begin the conversation.

People do recover from eating disorders, but almost all of those who do, need professional help to get back on track. We know this is hard, and we appreciate your courage as you take the first step by calling today to make an appointment with your physician or counsellor.

■ The above information is re-printed with kind permission from ANRED. Visit www.anred.com for more information.
© ANRED (Anorexia Nervosa and Related Eating Disorders, Inc.)

Associated mental health conditions and addictions

Below you will find some of the psychological illnesses and addictions that can sometimes coexist with an eating disorder

In people who suffer from eating disorders it is not uncommon to find other associated psych-ological disorders that coexist with their anorexia, bulimia and/or compulsive overeating. In some cases, their eating disorder is a secondary symptom to an underlying psychological disorder (such as some people who also suffer with multiple personality disorder), and in other cases, the psychological disorder may be secondary to the eating disorder (as with some people also suffering with depression). Men and women may also suffer from both an eating disorder and other psychological disorder(s) that completely coexist with one another... or they can suffer from an eating disorder and have little or no signs of an additional psychological disorder (note: the longer a person suffers, the more probable that they may be dealing with depression or anxiety as well). It is important to the recovery process and treatment that all these issues are addressed, and that a proper diagnosis be determined.

Some of the psychological illness that can be (but are not always) found in people suffering with anorexia, bulimia and compulsive

overeating are: obsessive compulsive disorder, depression, post-traumatic stress disorder, bipolar and bipolar II disorder, borderline personality disorder, panic disorders and anxiety, dissociative disorder and multiple personality disorder.

In addition, some people suffering with an eating disorder may also be exhibiting other addictive or self-destructive behaviours. As an eating disorder is a reaction to low self-esteem, and a negative means of coping with life and stress, so are other types of addictions. These can include alcoholism, drug addiction (illegal, prescription and/or over-the-counter medications), and self-injury, cutting and self-mutilation.

Harming oneself, also known as cutting, self-mutilation, or SIV (self-inflicted violence) is a coping mechanism that is sometimes found in people also suffering with an eating disorder. For some, they may find it easier to deal with real physical pain than to deal with their emotional pain, or some may feel emotionally numb and using SIV reminds them that they are alive. They may even feel that they deserve to be hurt. It can be used to block out emotional pain, or to make the person feel 'strong'. It is a way to cope with stress and anger, shame and guilt, sadness, and as a release for emotions that have built up inside. SIV can be

mild to severe, but it should never be confused with a conscious attempt to commit suicide (though some may die as a result of their actions, this is relatively uncommon). SIV can include cutting, burning, punching, slapping, hitting oneself with an object, eye-pushing, biting and head-banging, and less common methods would be those that have long-lasting or lifelong effects such as bone breaking, or amputation.

Suffering with an eating disorder, alone or combined with any other psychological illness or addiction, leaves each sufferer needing new and better ways to cope

---

Suffering with an eating disorder, alone or combined with any other psychological illness or addiction, leaves each sufferer needing new and better ways to cope.

There is an indication that eating disorders may sometimes coexist with ADD (attention deficit disorder) and ADHD (attention deficit hyperactivity disorder). Studies have shown that women who go

undiagnosed as ADD (but do in fact have it) are much more likely to develop an eating disorder. Some of the neurological symptoms of ADD/ADHD can be holding onto negative thoughts and/or anger, as well as impulsivity both verbally (interrupting others) and in actions (acting before thinking). There may also be unexplained emotional negativity, depression, and even attempted suicide. To get a proper diagnosis, there are whole criteria that need to be met.

From the National ADD Association, 'If untreated, individuals with ADHD may develop a variety of secondary problems as they move through life, including depression, anxiety, substance abuse, academic failure, vocational problems, marital discord, and emotional distress.' There are many of the same possible coexisting psychological illnesses with ADHD/ADD as with an eating disorder, including: depression, bipolar disorder, post-traumatic stress disorder, and obsessive compulsive disorder.

I have received email from a good number of men who are simultaneously living with ADHD and an eating disorder, and I suspect there are many more, both men and women, doing the same.

■ The above information is reprinted with kind permission from Something Fishy. Visit www.something-fishy.org for more information.

© *Something Fishy*

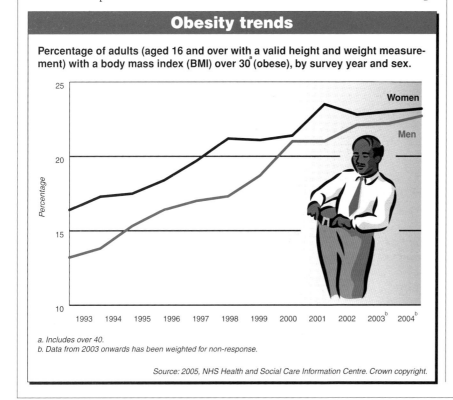

Obesity trends

Percentage of adults (aged 16 and over with a valid height and weight measurement) with a body mass index (BMI) over 30[a] (obese), by survey year and sex.

Women

Men

Percentage

25

20

15

10

1993 1994 1995 1996 1997 1998 1999 2000 2001 2002 2003[b] 2004[b]

a. Includes over 40.
b. Data from 2003 onwards has been weighted for non-response.

Source: 2005, NHS Health and Social Care Information Centre. Crown copyright.

Reflections of my former self

Katharine Wealthall tells how shattering anorexia is – and dispels some myths about the disease

I am an anorexic. I have anorexia nervosa.

What does that mean? According to some, it means being stick-thin like a model or Hollywood star; perhaps it is attention-seeking or maybe it means choosing to abuse body, mind and spirit all in the pursuit of size 8 jeans. Last week, new research suggested that elevated levels of antibodies attack the chemical messages that control appetite and consequently cause eating disorders. So, being anorexic simply means a loss of appetite caused by an infection! The reality is that having anorexia is like being lost in a black chasm, utterly helpless in the control of an invisible force, so overwhelming that you barely resemble the person you once were – or at least the person you wanted to be.

Anorexia is relentless; the mindset drives you to set standards which are, to the rational person, clearly unattainable. Failure is therefore inevitable. Living within the depths of anorexia is terrifying, confusing and totally beyond reason. Living in recovery is not always much easier.

Contrary to popular belief, anorexia and bulimia are not about food. I can sincerely state that I have never lost my appetite – indeed, part of the illness for me was to feel hunger and deny myself food as punishment. I did not allow myself to eat because I believed I didn't deserve to. Abusing food or depriving oneself of food are symptoms, the consequence of an illness so complex that after a lifetime with it, it is still impossible to fathom.

I have lived with anorexia all my life. I was 30 last month. Even though the obvious physical symptoms did not manifest until I was 13, the damaging thought processes were evident before that. When I was seven years old one of my guinea pigs died. I vividly remember carrying the remaining one round the garden telling her over and over again I was sorry and that I hadn't split them up on purpose. I felt so guilty, so responsible, I could not sleep or eat properly for weeks.

New research suggested that elevated levels of antibodies attack the chemical messages that control appetite and consequently cause eating disorders

When I was a teenager, and my parents, teachers and friends noticed I was losing weight, it was a whole lot longer before I would acknowledge it. The intensity of my feelings of failure and worthlessness grew. I believed I had no right to be alive and that if my parents really knew me, they wouldn't love me. Nothing made sense. The only place I felt safe, felt real, was when I was with my animals. Fuelled by the need to punish myself and the desire to disappear, I engaged in anorexic behaviours. I had a wide elastic belt I wore with my school uniform and every week I would cut a bit more off it. If I had not lost enough weight the belt would cut into me; if it fitted I would simply cut more off. My weight dropped to five stone and with it came the inevitable lies and secrecy, which increased my self-loathing. At the age of 14 I contemplated suicide; it was only my intense love for my animals that stopped me.

Throughout my adolescence, followed by four years of hell at Cambridge, my behaviour deteriorated to include induced vomiting, obsessive compulsive disorder, alcohol abuse and self-harm. Anorexia makes you into an incredibly unpleasant person and maintaining relationships was difficult. I felt that I was undeserving

of friends and so removed from normal life that I pushed people away.

And with no one to keep an eye on me, the anorexia took total control. Leaving my pony, the last of my beloved pets, the self-hatred intensified. The starvation of my teenage years did not occur again; it was more subtle than that. I believed I deserved to suffer but did not want to cause my family worry. I had to keep the illness secret. I developed a fixed routine regarding food; if I ate anything at all I would induce vomiting afterwards but at home at weekends I ate 'normally' (small amounts but enough to stop anyone asking questions). I continued at university with my days filled with rounds of self-abuse – I was the most ill I had ever been. It is a myth that a person has to be skeletal to be dangerously ill with an eating disorder; absolutely untrue.

In-patient treatment, in 1999, came just in time. After Pete (my pony) died suddenly in 1997, the condition hit me with a strength I had never experienced before. Even after 10 years of anorexia I had no idea it could be so all-consuming. I was physically, emotionally and mentally exhausted – and scared. I was certain that, if I did not receive real help, it would kill me.

Nothing could have prepared me for the fight needed to reach recovery. At times, living with the illness seemed easy by comparison. In hospital I had to allow myself to be broken down into little pieces and rebuilt. Discharge from hospital was so exciting because I genuinely believed I was cured. I understand now that life in recovery is management of the illness. Just as an alcoholic makes the daily decision not to drink, I make the daily decision to stay well.

There are strategies I use to achieve this. For example, I always have a plan so that I know exactly what I'm doing. If I have a structure to the day I know that I am not wasting time (a real source of panic for me) and if I have a productive day the risk of feeling a failure – a trigger that can give the illness strength – is eliminated. Every time a negative thought enters my head I have to counter it with a positive thought or action – anything can help, from saying something positive out loud to cuddling my dogs.

My relationship with food is still difficult. I feel guilty spending money on food and struggle with the idea that I am allowed to eat, especially foods that I would consider treats. I constantly ask my husband if it's OK for me to eat the amount on my plate. Every day in recovery is another day. It can be an immense struggle; there are times when allowing the illness to take over seems so appealing because the fight would be finished. But anorexia must not win; I simply cannot let it. I have so much to keep fighting for, I have my exceptional husband, wonderful family and dogs and am finally pursuing my lifelong dream of an acting career.

I have anorexia nervosa, I am an anorexic, but that is not all I am.

■ Katharine Wealthall's *Little Steps – Surviving Anorexia and Bulimia Nervosa* (Chipmunka) is published tomorrow (10 October 2005).
9 October 2005

© Katharine Wealthall

Anorexia could be physical, not mental

Eating disorders linked to infections which hit immune system

The eating disorders anorexia and bulimia may be biological diseases rather than mental conditions, experts said yesterday.

Research suggests they are linked to infections which disrupt the body's immune system, causing it to attack the chemicals in the brain controlling appetite.

This would put the disorders in the category of auto-immune diseases, which also includes rheumatoid arthritis and multiple sclerosis, in which the immune system turns on the body.

The findings, by a Swedish team at the Karolinska Institute in Stockholm, support evidence that eating disorders cannot be explained by psychiatric factors alone.

Other studies have shown that anorexia is eight times more likely to strike an individual if a close relative is anorexic and scientists have identified two genes that may be involved.

Experts hope the new results will help accelerate the search for potential treatments. Traditionally they have centred on psychotherapy, nutrition, and, in some cases, medication such as antidepressants.

In the latest study Professor Tomas Hokfelt and colleagues found that those with anorexia and bulimia had higher than usual levels of a particular group of antibodies. Antibodies are produced by the body's immune system to fight off foreign bacteria.

Professor Hokfelt says the chemicals the body produces to control appetite have important similarities to proteins found in the influenza A virus and in common bacteria such as e.coli.

He believes that when the body is infected by one of these, it produces antibodies to fight them off – but the same antibodies then go on to begin targeting molecules that control appetite.

Susan Ringwood, Chief Executive of the Eating Disorders Association, said: 'There is already research suggesting that eating disorders can follow an infection, so this is very interesting.'

Diana, Princess of Wales, described how she struggled with bulimia, bingeing on food before making herself sick.

Former Spice Girl Geri Halliwell has also fought bulimia and TV presenter Gail Porter has told of her battles with anorexia.

■ This article first appeared in the *Daily Mail*, 26 September 2005.
© 2006 Associated Newspapers Ltd

Bulimia

Information from NHS Direct

Introduction

Over 85% of reported cases of bulimia occur in girls in their late teens and early twenties. On average, bulimia occurs slightly later than anorexia nervosa. Approximately 10% of people with the condition are men.

Bulimia, medically known as bulimia nervosa, is marked by cycles of binge eating of excessive quantities of food, followed by purging using vomiting, laxatives or diuretics and/or excessive exercising.

If you have bulimia nervosa you are likely to be preoccupied with food. You may have episodes of craving food and eat vast amounts of food in secret. The common foods to binge on are sweet, high-calorie foods often thought of as 'treats' such as ice cream, cakes, chocolate and biscuits.

It is thought that bulimia nervosa is a physical way of dealing with depression, stress, or issues of self-esteem. It may protect you from experiencing feelings and emotions that have become distressing and intolerable. It enables feelings of short-lived control and calmness but the strategy soon becomes destructive as you begin to feel guilty, disgusted and out of control. This cycle of bingeing and purging maintains and increases the severity of the condition, which can come to dominate all your emotional experience.

The frequency of these bulimic cycles will vary. Some will binge and purge occasionally whilst others will binge and purge several times a day. Some cases of bulimia nervosa are short-lived. However, often the symptoms will be present for some months or years before help is sought. Sometimes bulimia persists for many years, and in some people symptoms may be present all their lives.

Over 85% of reported cases of bulimia occur in girls in their late teens and early twenties.
On average, bulimia occurs slightly later than anorexia nervosa

---

Sometimes in association with bulimia, other problems may be present, including drug abuse, alcohol abuse, self-harm, shoplifting and promiscuity. Also bulimia may be preceded by a brief period of anorexia nervosa and weight may remain low.

It is difficult to find accurate statistics about bulimia nervosa as it so often goes undiagnosed and untreated. The incidence is usually put at 0.5 to 1% of young women but the true incidence may be higher.

Symptoms

Physical symptoms of bulimia are:
- fluctuations in weight;
- sore throat, heartburn and tooth decay caused by excessive vomiting;
- puffiness of the face caused by swollen salivary glands;
- spots and poor skin condition;
- scarred knuckles due to attempts to force fingers down the throat to induce vomiting;
- irregular periods;
- lethargy and tiredness;
- depression, anxiety, low self-esteem and mood swings;
- constipation and intestinal damage.

Other signs:
- fear of obesity and distorted perception of body weight;
- obsession with eating and episodes of irresistible craving for food and secret bingeing;
- excessive exercise;
- fasting for periods of time;
- using laxatives, diuretics or enemas to counteract the bingeing;
- tendency to leave the table immediately after a meal and disappearing to the toilet in order to vomit food eaten.

Causes

The causes of bulimia nervosa remain largely unknown but possibilities include the following.
- Some people who develop this condition have been physically or sexually abused as children.
- Some people have been in difficult family or sexual relationships.
- Others appear not to have experienced these problems but still lack self-worth and need an outlet for their emotions.

- Research suggests there may be a genetic link.
- Social pressures to be thin to be sexually attractive may be a factor.

Diagnosis

People with bulimia are often of normal weight, so the condition is not easy to recognise by friends or family.

Common indications of bulimia are erosion of teeth enamel, enlarged salivary glands, scarring on the back of the hands, or swollen hands and feet (as a result of suddenly stopping taking laxatives or diuretics)

Common indications are erosion of teeth enamel, enlarged salivary glands, scarring on the back of the hands, or swollen hands and feet (as a result of suddenly stopping taking laxatives or diuretics). The person may have a history of anorexia, unhappiness with their weight, or may ask for help with weight loss. They might also complain of symptoms such as abdominal pain, bloating, constipation, irregular menstrual periods, or a sore swollen oesophagus (gullet).

Treatment

Severity of bulimia varies considerably. It is likely that there are large numbers of girls with mild symptoms who never seek medical help and do recover on their own. However, there is a risk that the bulimia will slowly get worse with time. A common time for women to seek help is when they are planning to start a family.

Guidelines for the treatment published by the National Institute for Clinical Excellence (NICE) in January 2004 sets the standard for NHS treatment of eating disorders in England and Wales.

The main guidelines for bulimia nervosa are as follows.

- GPs should make an early diagnosis of an eating disorder so those seeking help should be assessed and receive treatment at the earliest opportunity.
- Your assessment should be comprehensive and include physical, psychological and social needs.
- Your GP should initially offer you an evidence-based self-help programme. As an alternative or additional, adults with bulimia nervosa should be offered antidepressant medication – fluoxetine (selective serotonin re-uptake inhibitor/SSRI).
- If self-help does not work you should be offered cognitive behavioural therapy, especially developed for bulimia (CBT-BN). The course should normally be 16 to 20 individual sessions over four to five months.
- If you are a teenager with Bulimia you should be offered CBT-BN adapted as needed to suit your age, circumstances and level of development. Family members (including other children in the family) should be involved as appropriate. The course should normally be 16 to 20 individual sessions over four to five months.
- If you do not respond to or do not want CBT, other psychological treatment should be considered.
- You will normally be treated in an out-patient setting, however a very small minority of people with bulimia may need inpatient treatment, when the condition is linked to a suicide risk or severe self-harm.

Advice can also be sought from specialist eating disorder helplines. You may be encouraged to keep a diary of eating habits. Success often depends on you wanting to recover – if this is the case, the outcome of treatment is very good.

Complications

In extreme circumstances, even if you are of normal weight, you can severely damage your body by frequent bingeing and purging.

Erosion of the teeth is common, due to regular exposure of the teeth to stomach acid when vomiting. Being sick often can also lead to a swollen, irritated or torn oesophagus.

Electrolyte imbalance, dangerously low levels of the essential minerals and dehydration, can cause heart problems and, occasionally, sudden death due to a heart attack.

They may also cause severe problems to other vital internal organs of the body. In rare instances, bingeing can cause the stomach to rupture.

- The above information is reprinted with kind permission from NHS Direct. Visit www.nhsdirect.nhs.uk for more information.

© Crown copyright material is reproduced with the permission of the Controller of HMSO and Queen's Printer for Scotland

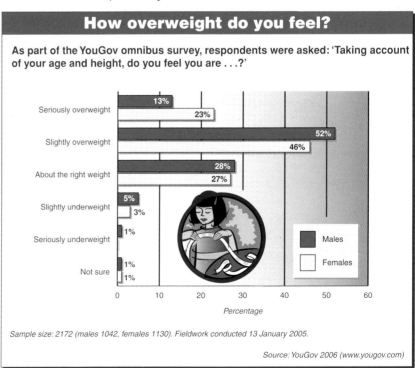

How overweight do you feel?

As part of the YouGov omnibus survey, respondents were asked: 'Taking account of your age and height, do you feel you are . . .?'

Seriously overweight — Males 13%, Females 23%
Slightly overweight — Males 52%, Females 46%
About the right weight — Males 28%, Females 27%
Slightly underweight — Males 5%, Females 3%
Seriously underweight — Males 1%, Females 1%
Not sure — Males 1%, Females 1%

Percentage

Males
Females

Sample size: 2172 (males 1042, females 1130). Fieldwork conducted 13 January 2005.

Source: YouGov 2006 (www.yougov.com)

Binge eating

Information from NHS Direct

Introduction

Food is important for growth and development, but we do not always eat to satisfy our hunger. Most of us overeat from time to time, and we may feel bloated or excessively full as a result. Occasional over-indulgence does not constitute an eating disorder, and binge eating has only recently been recognised as an eating disorder in its own right.

Binge eating is a mental disorder, but it is also triggered by the effect that overeating has on the body

Binge eating is characterised by a sense of having lost control over eating. People with the disorder may find themselves eating large quantities of food even when not hungry, usually in a short period of time. This is accompanied by feelings of guilt or disgust at the perception of having consumed so much. The self-loathing binge eaters feel when they overeat highlights underlying psychological issues that are often both a cause and an effect of the disorder.

Binge eaters often eat until they are uncomfortably full. In this sense, the disorder is similar to bulimia nervosa, another eating disorder in which large quantities of food are consumed rapidly. However, bulimics then 'purge' the food they have eaten through self-induced vomiting or by taking laxatives. People who binge eat do not purge themselves, and feel ashamed of their behaviour whether overweight or not.

Binge eating is a mental disorder, but it is also triggered by the effect that overeating has on the body. Binge eating causes a surge of blood glucose, which stimulates the pancreas into producing insulin – a hormone naturally produced by the body to regulate the amount of glucose in the blood. This means that after the initial 'high', blood sugar levels actually fall rapidly, which sends a false message to the brain that we need more food in order to top up glucose levels. Cravings for sugary foods that will provide a quick glucose 'fix' continue, and binge eaters may therefore consume large quantities of food even when not hungry.

Symptoms

The primary symptom of binge eating is weight gain, and many people suffering from attacks of binge eating are already seriously overweight. People carrying too much weight are vulnerable to other health problems associated with obesity, including:

- high cholesterol levels;
- high blood pressure;
- diabetes;
- gallbladder disease; and
- heart disease.

Aside from weight gain, the physical effects on the body caused by fluctuating blood sugar levels are:

- cravings;
- stomach pains;
- intolerance to heat and cold;
- headaches.

People who binge eat are unable to comprehend why they cannot control their body's sugar cravings, and become trapped in a cycle of bingeing – guilt – restraint – bingeing. People who binge eat blame themselves for their weakness, and reduce their sense of self-esteem even further. Binge eating may cause associated psychological problems of:

- depression;
- panic attacks;
- lack of concentration;
- hopelessness; and
- anxiety.

Causes

There is no one cause for binge eating, but like most eating disorders, it is generally seen as a way of coping with feelings of unhappiness, depression and low self-esteem. Media and societal pressure to achieve a slim body shape may fuel the guilty feelings people experience

CRAVE

BINGE

GUILT

in relation to food. Attempts to lose weight that are motivated by a negative body image and sense of inadequacy frequently lead to reactive overeating when the desired body shape cannot be achieved. Obesity, whether real or perceived, and pressure from others to lose weight can cause the tendency to binge eat to develop.

Certain personality types, such as givers, helpers, worriers and pleasers may be susceptible to binge eating. Jobs that require weight control, or place people in a food environment, may also trigger binge eating.

It is important to get help quickly if you feel you may have an eating disorder

---

Stress is another common trigger of eating disorders. Moving house, job, or school, or the death of a friend or relative, are events that are often linked to eating problems.

Eating disorders are a physical display of the difficulties a person may be experiencing in their personal life. Binge eaters often feel ashamed at the volume of food they consume, and may feel that their lack of control around food mirrors the lack of control they have over their personal lives.

Diagnosis

Binge eating is hard to diagnose because it can take so many forms. People who binge eat may feel depressed and panicky after eating one chocolate bar too many, or continually pick at food throughout the day, even after meals and when full up.

The signs of binge eating are:
- lack of control over eating;
- consuming a large amount of food in a short period of time (around two hours);
- eating much faster than normal during a binge;
- eating until feeling uncomfortably full;
- eating a large amount of food even when not hungry;
- eating alone or secretly due to embarrassment about the amount of food being consumed; and
- feelings of guilt, shame, or disgust after overeating.

People who eat in this way over a long period of time, say six months, may be diagnosed as having a binge eating disorder.

Treatment

It is important to get help quickly if you feel you may have an eating disorder. Your doctor will assess you, and advise the best course of treatment to deal with the problem. Dieting as a means of dealing with the problem should be avoided, particularly if you are not overweight, as this may make the binge eating worse.

People who are overweight should follow a weight-loss plan drawn up by a health care professional, but underlying psychological issues usually need to be dealt with first if weight loss is to be successful and lasting.

Guidance issued in 2004 by the National Institute of Clinical Excellence (NICE) recommends a self-help programme, under the supervision of health care profe-ssionals. Cognitive behavioural therapy and other psychological treatments should be offered, and in some cases treatment with an SSRI-type of antidepressant may be required at the same times as, or instead of, talking therapies.

People who binge are encouraged to stop relying on the cycle of bingeing and guilt as a way of dealing with emotional problems. It is possible to recover fully from eating disorders, and certain forms of therapy may help such as:
- counselling;
- self-help and support groups;
- psychotherapy (drama or arts therapy); and
- diet and nutritional advice.

Prevention

It is important to understand the effect of low blood sugar levels on the body, and the food cravings it causes. Keeping a food diary may help to highlight when you binge, and the types of food you are eating that trigger a rapid and false sense of hunger.

Eating food that is low in sugar will provide a slow and sustained energy release throughout the day. Eating little and often, including complex carbohydrates to fill you up, will also help. Cutting out alcohol, caffeine, and sugary foods will prevent the yo-yo effect on the body's blood sugar levels.

■ The above information is reprinted with kind permission from NHS Direct. Please visit www.nhsdirect.nhs.uk for more information.

© Crown copyright material is reproduced with the permission of the Controller of HMSO and Queen's Printer for Scotland

Other types of eating disorders

Information from Something Fishy

Pica

Pica, a widely misunderstood phenomenon, is defined as a compulsive craving for eating, chewing or licking non-food items or foods containing no nutrition. These can include such things as chalk, plaster, paint chips, baking soda, starch, glue, rust, ice, coffee grounds, and cigarette ashes. It may sometimes be linked to certain mineral deficiencies (i.e. iron or zinc). Pica can be associated with, developmental delays, mental deficiencies and/or a family history of the disorder. There may be psychological disturbances that lead to pica as well, such as conditions in which a child lives in a low-income or poor family, or who lives in an environment of little love and support.

Because of the inherent danger in eating non-food items, it is extremely important that an individual suffering with pica be evaluated by a doctor, given the correct diagnosis, and treated promptly. The treatment that will follow will depend on the causes of the behaviour. If the compulsion is driven by a vitamin or mineral deficiency, supplements will be prescribed. Examination of the home environment, behaviour-modification therapy and psychological treatment may also be needed.

Pica is fairly common in pregnant women and symptoms usually disappear following the birth of the child.

Complications of pica can include lead poisoning, malnutrition, abdominal problems, intestinal obstruction, hypokalemia, hyperkalemia, mercury poisoning, phosphorus intoxication, and dental injury.

It may be possible (but uncommon) for people with anorexia and/or bulimia to develop pica because of the compulsive nature of these illnesses to binge, and/or the malnutrition that can set in. If the two disorders coexist, it is important to tell your doctor of both.

Pica is defined as a compulsive craving for eating, chewing or licking non-food items or foods containing no nutrition

---

Prader-Willi syndrome

Prader-Willi syndrome is a congenital condition (present at birth) and is believed to be caused by an abnormality in the genes that occurs (though statistically it does not seem to run in families). Children born with Prader-Willi syndrome may have early feeding difficulties that lead to tube feeding, and often have a degree of behavioural and/or mental problems (some severe).

The person with Prader-Willi syndrome has an insatiable appetite. This can lead to obesity, stealing, and eating pet foods and items that are spoiled. This continuous appetite is caused by a defect in the hypothalamus – a part of the brain that regulates hunger – that causes the person to never actually feel full. There may be sleep disorders and abnormalities, bouts of rage, a higher threshold for pain, compulsive behaviours such as picking at the skin, and even psychoses.

Physical problems associated with Prader-Willi syndrome can be delayed motor development, abnormal growth, speech impairments, stunted sexual development, poor muscle tone, dental problems, obesity and diabetes type-II. The life expectancy of a person with Prader-Willi syndrome may be normal if weight is controlled.

Prader-Willi syndrome is a rare condition that puts a great deal of stress on the families involved. It is important to get the proper diagnosis early and to find medical and emotional support.

Night eating syndrome (NES)

Here's the *Merck Manual* definition and conclusion about treatment. (1982 ed.) page 917: 'Night Eating

Syndrome consists of morning anorexia, evening hyperphagia (abnormally increased appetite for consumption of food frequently associated with injury to the hypothalamus) and insomnia. Attempts at weight reduction in these two conditions, (referring to bulimia as well), are usually unsuccessful and may cause the patient unnecessary distress.'

The authors call both syndromes, 'deviant eating patterns apparently based on stress and emotional disturbance'.

Episodes of anorexia and insomnia can begin at an early age, usually in children who are overweight, and are sometimes accompanied by joint pain. It is interesting to note what the parent of a now 24-year-old daughter had to say:

'I've always had the feeling that much of the stress and emotional disturbances my daughter has suffered have been the result of social rejection and discrimination rather than the cause of her eating disorder ... more so as she got older. She started out as an intelligent, outgoing, cheerful human being. There is a line in our culture where a marginally acceptable "chubby" child becomes a miserable adolescent and then a depressed adult.'

People with night eating syndrome are characterised as people that put off eating until late in the day, who binge on food in the evenings and who experience problems with falling asleep and/or staying asleep.

'People who exhibit NES don't eat a lot at one sitting, often skip breakfast, and don't start eating until noon,' says psychiatrist Albert Stunkard, an obesity researcher at the University of Pennsylvania. 'They will over eat the rest of the day, and eat frequently. They also have difficulty falling asleep or staying asleep.'

Sleep eating disorder (SED-NOS)

Sleep eating disorder typically falls into the category of sleep disorders, though it is a combined sleep-eating problem. Sufferers tend to be overweight and have episodes of recurrent sleep-walking, during which time they binge on usually large quantities of food, often high in sugar or fat. Most often, sufferers do not remember these episodes, putting them at great risk of unintentional self-injury.

Because of the compulsive nature of this illness, sufferers are at the same physical health risks as those of compulsive overeaters with the added risks of sleep-walking. It is not uncommon to find a person suffering to be anxious, tired, stressed and angry.

People with night eating syndrome are characterised as people that put off eating until late in the day, who binge on food in the evenings and who experience problems with falling asleep

---

Eating and/or sleeping problems
It is important to be aware that throughout life, during positive and negative stress periods, people may experience eating and/or sleep pattern problems. If either or both of these conditions persist or interfere with daily life, then it is important to identify the underlying cause(s) of the problem. Problems with eating and sleeping are defined as usually over/under eating or too much or too little sleep. During the past decade, we have become aware of the detrimental effects of anorexia, bulimia and compulsive overeating and while these problems may warrant medical attention, the underlying causes need to be identified and appropriate coping skills developed.

Body dysmorphic disorder

BDD, or body dysmorphic disorder, is a preoccupation or obsession with a defect in visual appearance, whether that be an actual slight imperfection or an imagined one. An example of this would be obsessing to the point of severe depression (sometimes including thoughts about or attempts at suicide) over physical attributes such as freckles, a large nose, blotchy skin, wrinkles, acne or scarring, though the preoccupation can include any part of the body. Areas of the face and head, specifically the skin, hair and nose, are most common.

People suffering with BDD may often have low self-esteem and unreasonable fears of rejection from others due to their perceived ugliness. Some sufferers realise that their perception of the 'defect' is distorted, but find the impulse to think about it uncontrollable.

There are two types of BDD – the non-delusional type and the delusional type (where the person actually has hallucinations of a completely imagined defect, or an imagined gross exaggeration of a small defect). The delusional form is less common and more severe.

Men and women living with BDD may practise unusually compulsive rituals to look at, hide, cover and/or improve their defect(s). They may spend a great deal of time looking at themselves in anything mirror-like and trying to convince others of how ugly they are. They may be compulsive in searching out doctors to treat them with medications and/or plastic surgery. Patients may go to any lengths to improve their appearance, including using methods that are dangerous. Some may even attempt their own surgery, or commit suicide.

Mental illnesses that sometimes co-exist with BDD are depression, obsessive-compulsive disorder (OCD) and social phobia.

Treatment is often difficult, but there has been progress shown with medications such as Prozac, and cognitive-behaviour therapy. Diagnosis can often be difficult because of the patients' shame (causing them to keep their symptoms a secret). Symptoms as per the DSM-IV (from Mental Health Net) are:

- preoccupation with an imagined defect in appearance. If a slight physical anomaly is present, the person's concern is markedly excessive;
- the preoccupation causes clinically significant distress or impairment in social, occupational, or other important areas of functioning;

Orthorexia nervosa is an obsession with a 'pure' diet, where it interferes with a person's life. It becomes a way of life filled with chronic concern for the quality of food being consumed

---

- the preoccupation is not better accounted for by another mental disorder (e.g., dissatisfaction with body shape and size in anorexia nervosa).

Orthorexia nervosa

It should be noted that orthorexia nervosa is not a condition that a physician will diagnose, as there is no clinical guideline for this disorder. It is a condition that has been observed as an extreme pattern of dietary purity and has not yet been defined under the clinical diagnostic manual (DSM-IV).

Orthorexia nervosa is an obsession with a 'pure' diet, where it interferes with a person's life. It becomes a way of life filled with chronic concern for the quality of food being consumed. When the person suffering with orthorexia nervosa slips up from wavering from their 'perfect' diet, they may resort to extreme acts of further self-disipline

including even stricter regimens and fasting.

'This transference of all of life's value into the act of eating makes orthorexia a true disorder. In this essential characteristic, orthorexia bears many similarities to the two well-known eating disorders anorexia and bulimia. Where the bulimic and anorexic focus on the quantity of food, the orthorexic fixates on its quality. All three give food an excessive place in the scheme of life.' (Steven Bratman, M.D., October 1997).

As noted by BeyondVeg.com, orthorexia nervosa should only be characterised when it is in the long-term (paying attention to healthy food for a few weeks where it becomes a normal and healthy routine not obsessed over, would not be considered a disorder), when it has a significant negative impact on an individual's life (thinking about food to avoid the stresses of life, thinking about how food is prepared to avoid negative emotions, thinking about food the majority of each individual's day), and where food rituals are not better explained by something like religious rites (such as in the Orthodox Jewish religion).

Bigorexia

It should be noted that bigorexia is not a condition that a physician will diagnose, as there is currently no clinical guideline for this disorder. It is a condition that has recently been observed by several psychiatrists as the 'opposite of anorexia'.

Found typically in body-building circles and known as muscle dysmorphia or reverse anorexia, bigorexia is a condition in which the sufferer is constantly worried that they are too small. This goes beyond the typical body-building gym-goer, and transcends into dangerous realms when men and women are willing to go to all lengths to increase muscle mass. Dr Harrison Pope, of the McLean Hospital, says, 'There's nothing inherently pathological about being an avid gym-goer, but it shouldn't take over your life.' In likening bigorexia to anorexia he comments, 'They are both disorders of body image, the preoccupations simply go in opposite directions.'

Muscle dysmorphia isn't as acutely life-threatening as starving yourself, Pope says, but its sufferers are more likely to take other risks with their health, such as using steroids or other body-building drugs. One muscle dysmorphic woman was hospitalised for kidney failure brought on by her high-protein diet and steroid use. Within months of her release from the hospital, she was back on the drugs and unhealthy diet (ABC News, Claudine Chamberlain).

Harrison Pope and several other researchers put together this set of criteria for diagnosing muscle dysmorphia.

1. The person is preoccupied with the idea that their body is not lean and muscular. They spend long hours lifting weights and pay excessive attention to diet.
2. This preoccupation causes major distress or impairs the person's social or professional life. The person may forego important social, work-related or recreational activities. They may avoid situations where their body will be exposed. The person continues to work out or diet even when they know it could hurt their health or well-being.
3. The focus of the person's concerns is on being too small or not muscular enough, as opposed to concerns about being fat.

- The above information is reprinted with kind permission from Something Fishy. Visit www.something-fishy.org for more information.

© *Something Fishy*

Eating problems

Information taken from a ChildLine information sheet

'I'm not very happy today. Woke up feeling OK then helped my mum with the shopping and bought a lot of binge food. Came home and ate the lot. Went to throw it up, but I really did not have the energy and my throat hurt from yesterday, so I only threw up once.

'Then I went to the swimming pool and swam 140 lengths. I've had my head down the toilet every morning, afternoon and evening. Feel complete and utter rubbish, but wore my smile, so everyone left me alone.' Laura, 16

Many young people experience difficulties with eating food at some time in their lives. These can range from not liking foods (which happens to most people) to clinical eating disorders. It is estimated that as many as 1.15 million people in Britain suffer with an eating problem. Approximately 90,000 people are thought to be receiving treatment for either anorexia or bulimia.

ChildLine speaks to over 1,000 young people about an eating problem each year: 99 out of 100 callers are girls. Of those who give their age, we know that most are between 13 and 16 years old. But children as young as 10 and 11 years have phoned ChildLine to talk about eating problems, as well as older teenagers aged 17 and 18.

What are the most common eating problems?

Anorexia nervosa

'I have stopped eating. My teachers and my mum are always telling me off about it. It's the only part of my life I feel in control of. I might have to go into hospital as I haven't eaten for a couple of weeks. Mum just tries to make me eat more and so then I eat less.' Iris, 13

People with anorexia nervosa avoid eating and lose a lot of weight. In extreme cases, they can lose as much as two stone or 13kg in one month. People with anorexia often feel fat, even when they are very thin. They may use other ways of staying thin, such as exercising too much. They often hide food and follow very complicated plans to avoid food and appear heavier than they really are. Anorexia sufferers can become very weak and, without special help, some may even die.

When young people feel that they have very little control of the events going on around them, an eating problem can make them feel more in control

---

Bulimia nervosa

'I can just start eating something small, but then as I eat it, something inside me snaps and... I eat so much. After I've [thrown up and] cleared away the mess and all the food wrappers, I feel so much better, like I've been cleansed – because there's no food inside of me. But I also feel very tired, faint and sometimes tearful.' Laura, 16

Bulimia nervosa is when people binge and then make themselves sick to get rid of the food. Some people with bulimia and anorexia also use laxatives. These give you diarrhoea when taken in large doses. People with bulimia may not look overweight or underweight, which can make the problem difficult to recognise.

Repeated bingeing and purging (vomiting and/or taking laxatives) will eventually do serious damage to the body and can be very dangerous.

Compulsive eating

'I'm 13 stone and I want to lose weight, but I need to eat. I get so hungry. I want to be thin so that people will stop calling me names.' Darren, 8

Compulsive eating is when people eat much more than their bodies need over a long period, or use food to comfort or distract themselves. This can lead to being overweight and to serious medical problems, like heart problems or diabetes.

How do eating problems begin?

Many of the children and young people who talk to ChildLine about eating problems have low self-esteem or live in stressful family situations. Any number of other issues can 'trigger' an eating problem. Often young people tell us about a mixture of problems, such as pressure to be thin, bullying, abuse or the death of someone close.

When young people feel that they have very little control of the events going on around them, an eating problem can make them feel more in control. Without help, the eating problem itself can get out of control. It can damage people's bodies and can leave them feeling unhappy and bad about themselves and others, depressed, and even suicidal.

Callers to ChildLine range from those who are beginning to feel worried about the amount they eat, to a smaller number who may have had an eating disorder for several years, which has made them very ill. ChildLine listens to them all.

Many young people deny their eating problem or try to keep it a secret. But the sooner they accept that they have a problem, the easier it is to help. Help can include anything from talking to friends, family or a confidential counsellor, such as ChildLine, to seeing a doctor or spending time in hospital.

It is important to understand that an eating disorder is not really about food and it is therefore not appropriate to encourage someone with an eating disorder to 'eat up'. The eating problem is often a mask for other issues, so making the symptoms better for now may not help in the long run.

What do young people tell ChildLine about their eating problems?

Sarah told a ChildLine counsellor that she started to eat a lot under the pressure of exams. She put on weight and this led to her being teased and called names. She became very embarrassed about her size and said that one of the things that helped most was to talk to someone who couldn't see her.

Niri, 15, was doing well at school, had lots of friends and belonged to a drama group; then her family moved to another part of the country. Niri developed anorexia as a way of

expressing how very upset she felt about the move.

Jon phoned ChildLine over many months. He was having medical treatment for bulimia and the whole of his life felt out of control. He told ChildLine that he started bingeing and vomiting after he had been sexually abused. He said, 'There is something bad inside me that I need to get out.' Jon said that talking to ChildLine helped him to feel more in control of his life and happier about himself.

How can ChildLine help?

ChildLine counsellors listen without blaming or criticising. They take young people's problems seriously.

It can be easier to talk on the phone than face-to-face, especially at first. ChildLine counsellors will go at the caller's pace, and will not force the caller to talk about anything they don't want to.

Supportive family and friends are important, but it often helps to talk to someone who is not personally involved.

Young people can write or phone, and can phone just once or arrange to speak regularly to the same counsellor over a period of time.

ChildLine can advise children and young people about their eating problem.

ChildLine takes children and young people's problems seriously, giving them a chance to talk in confidence about their concerns, however large or small. ChildLine counsellors can also tell them where to go for more information, including local sources of help and advice. This service is free and available 24 hours a day, seven days a week.

Further information and advice

Publications
- *Anorexia Nervosa and Bulimia: How to Help*, Marilyn Duker and Roger Slade, Open University Press.
- *Anorexia Nervosa and Related Eating Disorders in Childhood and Adolescence*, Bryan Lask and Rachel Bryant-Waugh, Psychology Press.
- *Anorexia Nervosa: A Survival Guide for Families, Friends and Sufferers*, Janet Treasure, Psychology Press.
- *Anorexia Nervosa: The Wish to*

Change, A. H. Crisp, Neil Joughin, Christine Halek, Carol Bowyer, Psychology Press.
- *Bulimia Nervosa – A Guide to Recovery*, Peter Cooper and Christopher Fairburn, Constable Robinson.
- *Bulimia Nervosa: Getting Better Bit(e) by Bit(e): A Survival Kit for Sufferers of Bulimia Nervosa and Binge Eating Disorders*, Ulrich Schmidt and Janet Treasure, Psychology Press.
- *Eating Disorders. A Parent's Guide*, Bryan Lask and Rachel Bryant-Waugh, Penguin.
- *I'm in Control: Calls to ChildLine about Eating Disorders*, Brigid Mc-Conville, ChildLine, London, published June 2003.
- *It's Not About Food, It's About Feelings: An Educational Resource About Eating Disorders and Re-lated Issues, for Teachers and Youth Workers*, Eating Disorders Association.
- *What Works with Children and Adolescents? A Critical Review of Psychological Interventions with Children, Adolescents and their Families*, Alan Carr, Routledge.
- *Working with Eating Disorders and Self-Esteem*, Alex Yellowlees, Heinemann Educational.

Eating Disorders Association
103 Prince of Wales Road, Norwich, Norfolk NR1 1DW
Website: www.edauk.com
Adult helpline: 0845 634 1414
Monday to Friday 8.30am to 8.30pm
Saturday 1.00pm to 4.30pm
Email: helpmail@edauk.com
Youth helpline (for children and young people aged 18 or under): 0845 634 7650
Monday to Friday 4.00pm to 6.30pm
Saturday 1.00pm to 4.30pm
Youthline email: talkback@edauk.com
Youthline text service: 07 977 493 345
Textphone service (for people with impaired hearing): 01603 753322
Monday to Friday 8.30am to 8.30pm.

- The above information is re-printed with kind permission from ChildLine. Visit www.childline.org.uk for more information. ChildLine and the NSPCC joining together for children.
  © NSPCC

What have eating disorders got to do with puberty?

Information from the Eating Disorders Association

We know that puberty is a time when many young people may become affected by serious eating problems. We don't want this to happen to you and that's why we have written this article. We want to tell you how puberty can bring changes to your body shape and talk about why you might feel uncomfortable with your body. We also tell you a little about eating disorders and feeling good about yourself.

So what is puberty?

Puberty comes from the Latin word 'Pubertas', which means grown-up or adult. It's the word given to all of the changes that you go through from a child to an adult.

> *We are constantly bombarded with magazine items about losing weight and adverts for slimming plans or products. Some make claims that are almost impossible to achieve and may even be dangerous*

We don't all develop at the same speed or in the same way, and it's quite likely that you will grow outwards before you grow upwards: some people call this 'puppy fat'.

If you are a girl:

- you will grow taller more quickly;
- your breasts will start to swell, and may be tender;
- your body shape will become more round and curvy – you will notice it, especially on your hips;
- you will begin to grow body hair;
- your periods will also start at around this stage;
- you will probably get spots too and will probably have to start using deodorant.

Puberty for girls can begin as early as nine years old, but some girls don't start until they are 17 years old.

If you are a boy:

- you will grow much taller more quickly;
- your penis and testicles will grow larger;
- you will develop body hair;
- you will start to grow hair on your face and you might need to shave;
- you will have your first wet dream;
- your voice will break (becoming deeper);
- your muscles will develop and your chest and shoulders will get broader;
- you might find yourself being clumsier that usual;
- you will probably get spots too and have to start using deodorant.

Boys generally go through puberty a little later than girls. Adolescence and puberty doesn't only mean changes in your body – you are growing up as a person too. You are likely to want to be more independent and think about what sort of person you want to be and how you would like others to see you. You are likely to want more control over your life and the things you do than you have had before. Sometimes you may feel good about yourself and other times you may feel awful. You may have quick mood changes, laughing one minute and crying the next. Try not to worry, as you get older you will find these feelings easier to cope with.

Natural body shapes

'Eat it all up and you'll be big and strong.'

You may think that by eating in a certain way, you can change the shape of your body. However, a person's natural body shape is mostly based upon genes from parents and grandparents. It is important to realise that you cannot change your basic body shape. Most people are one of the following shapes.

Ectomorph

Tall and slim, strong bone structure, long legs and oval faces, don't gain weight easily, weight gain is distributed evenly over the body.

Mesomorph

Pear-shaped, larger hips and legs, weight tends to collect on hips, thighs and bottom, square or oval faces.

Endomorph

Apple-shaped, more weight on stomach, long body and shorter legs, large breasts and round faces, light bone structure, gains weight more easily than others.

It's also perfectly normal to be a mixture of all the above shapes. Just remember that we are all different and come in all shapes and sizes. Be proud of who you are.

People will notice how my body is changing!

You may feel embarrassed and sensitive about the changes that are happening to your body at this time and may feel heavy and overweight. This can make you feel unhappy and confused; especially as puberty itself brings lots of emotions to the surface. You could feel very vulnerable and upset. Sadly, there are people around who may use this as a chance to bully and tease you. You may feel anxious or depressed and start to feel bad about yourself and to worry about how you look. But bullying is never acceptable behaviour, so if you do experience problems with people picking on you and making you feel bad, please speak to somebody about it – maybe a parent, carer, schoolteacher or nurse, counsellor or Connexions advisor. Remember, you should never feel bullied or pressurised into losing weight.

But what if I still think I need to lose weight?
If you are still really concerned or feel unhappy about your weight then you would be best off talking to an adult you trust like a parent or carer, or a medical professional like your doctor or maybe the school nurse. Don't try and diet on your own, you could end up cutting out some of the foods and energy that your body most needs.

'Every time I open a magazine, I see lots of girls who are thinner than me!'
Problems with food are usually related to how you feel about yourself. You may see pictures of slim people in magazines who seem to be glamorous, powerful, happy and successful. You might even think that if you are very slim, then you will be happy and successful, but of course in real life the way someone looks has nothing to do with what they are really like inside.

We are constantly bombarded with magazine items about losing weight and adverts for slimming plans or products. Some make claims that are almost impossible to achieve and may even be dangerous. A lot of diet products seem to claim to be able to change your life, they may make you think that weight is the answer to everything – but of course it isn't.

It is important to remember that not everything we see on TV, read on the web, hear on the radio and see in the newspapers and magazines is true. Even photographs can be easily altered digitally. These days it can be quite difficult to work out what is the truth and what isn't.

What is healthy eating?
Healthy eating is about making sure your body gets the food it needs in order to work properly. We need the nutrients and energy in food to live. Food gives us energy and fuel for:
- growth;
- mental activity – including thinking and memory;
- physical activity;
- looking after your body and repairing it after you have been ill or injured;
- caring for your muscles – including your heart.

Healthy eating is not about skipping meals, eating less or cutting out everything you like. If you try to do this your body goes into starvation mode and actually stores what you do eat as fat, rather than using it as energy! If you don't eat enough and become hungry, a cycle of dieting then overeating can occur. Everyone needs to eat regularly.

A healthy diet is one with plenty of variety, that includes all of the food groups:
- carbohydrates such as bread, cereal, pasta, rice and potatoes. It is really important to keep carbohydrates in your diet because they provide you with essential nutrients and energy;
- protein such as meat, fish, beans, eggs, cheese, lentils and vegetable protein like tofu and quorn – these provide most of our energy;
- dairy foods such as butter, cheese and yoghurt;
- fruit and vegetables – five portions a day are recommended;
- foods containing fat and sugar – we all need both fat and sugar in our diets. Fat keeps our bodies functioning. Vitamins A, D and K can only dissolve in fat.

Many people sometimes don't eat breakfast because they have got up late; they don't feel like it; or because they think that skipping a meal will help them to lose weight. But breakfast really is the most important meal of the day. If you don't eat breakfast then your body will be very hungry and crave carbohydrates, and you are likely to find it difficult to control your eating for the rest of the day. You will also find it difficult to concentrate on anything other than food. If you miss meals you are more likely to binge. A binge is when someone eats as much as possible, in a short space of time, sometimes not at mealtimes.

'Your body needs nurturing during the teenage years.'

'Eat regularly and eat enough.'

'Weight control is not easy – it is not simply a case of eating less to lose weight.'

'There is no such thing as unhealthy food – only an unhealthy diet.'

There are no easy answers to the question of how much you should weigh. It is important to consider your age, height and body shape. We are all unique. It is important that you weigh enough for your body to function properly.

'Many people think that being too thin is healthier than being too fat – but both can be very dangerous to your health.'

If you don't get enough nourishment it can lead to many problems. These include stunted growth and brittle bones, and if you are a girl, your periods may stop and you may not be able to have a baby later in life.

What about exercise?
Some people who are worried about their weight do too much exercise to try to lower their weight. Exercise, in moderation, is good for you, but only if you are receiving the right amount of food and nutrients.

What is an eating disorder?

There are three main types of eating disorder: anorexia nervosa, bulimia nervosa and binge eating disorder. People with anorexia limit the amount of food they eat by skipping meals and rigidly controlling what they will and will not eat. Their concern about food, weight and calories can start to control them and they can become very ill. People with bulimia will also constantly think about food, but they become caught in a cycle of eating large amounts of food and then making themselves sick (or 'purging', as doctors call it), in order to try and lose the calories they have eaten. People with binge eating disorder will eat large amounts of food in a short period of time and tend to put on weight. There are also other eating disorders that are a mixture of the disorders above.

Are eating disorders just about food and weight?

No, they are about how we feel inside too. Eating disorders are a way of coping with feelings that are making you unhappy or depressed.

I haven't got an eating disorder, so what's the problem?

It's not unusual for young people to experiment with food. You may have decided to become a vegetarian, or to try out new and more exotic foods, for example. Maybe you have also tried changing your diet to improve your health? All of this, within reason, is OK and part of growing up.

However, some eating patterns can be damaging. Problems with food begin when it is used to cope with those times when you are bored, anxious, angry, lonely, ashamed or sad. Food becomes a problem when it is used to help you to cope with painful situations or feelings or relieving stress. If this is how you deal with food and you are unhappy about it, then you should talk about it with someone you trust. Try not to bottle up your feelings because this is not helpful to you or other people around you, it won't make you feel any better and the problem will not go away.

If you have a school nurse or school counsellor, then it might be a good idea to talk to them about how you are feeling. You could also phone the Eating Disorders Association's Youthline (0845 634 7650) and we would be happy to talk to you, or you can email us (talkback@edauk. com).

What is self-esteem?

Self-esteem is the way we feel about ourselves. Self-esteem means valuing your own worth and importance; not just when you get full marks in a test, not just when you are 'thin enough', and not just when you have a whole week doing everything that you are told to do – but all of the time! It is about having realistic expectations for ourselves – not aiming for something which we can never get to and then criticising ourselves for it.

It's not unusual for young people to experiment with food

You may not be very happy with yourself and feel that being thinner is the answer, but it isn't. We have to try and change the way we feel about ourselves from the inside. For example, feeling better about yourself for the whole person you are, rather than just the size you are.

'Self-esteem cannot be permanently raised by dieting or weight loss.'

There are many things which you might experience whilst growing up that could make you doubt yourself, your self-worth and your abilities. They may include:

- abuse;
- losing someone special;
- parents and/or family problems;
- moving house or school;
- bullying;
- problem 'friends';
- exams.

Even without these problems, the change from childhood to adulthood is stressful and can make you feel generally 'not good enough' and perhaps very confused about who you are and what sort of person you want to be. These feelings will get easier as you get older.

Trying to feel better about yourself and raise your self-esteem is not easy and takes a long time. Very often it helps to talk about how you feel with someone you trust: a member of your family; a friend; a person at school or a counsellor. Counsellors are trained people who can help you to work out why you are feeling upset or bad about yourself. We have information about counselling agencies for young people which are often free of charge and confidential, so if you would like to know if there is one near you, then please contact the Eating Disorders Association's Youthline.

There are some things that you could try now to start feeling better about yourself. Try to:

- think about what you're good at and give yourself praise for it;
- be proud of yourself, your skills and achievements;
- remember you are a worthwhile person;
- talk to others you trust about how you feel;
- talk about the things you find difficult;
- talk about difficult feelings with people you trust;
- be good to yourself and treat yourself as special.

Hopefully, this information has helped answer some of the questions which may have worried you. If you have any more questions or need to talk to someone, please contact us. Take care.

- The above information is re-printed with kind permission from the Eating Disorders Association. Visit www.edauk.com for more information.

© Eating Disorders Association

Time to tell

Young people affected by eating disorders speak out

- **45% of young people feel they couldn't tell anyone about their eating disorder.**
- **62% waited more than six months before they sought help.**
- **'I had continual arguments with my family that I was fine, I wasn't. I was dying.'**

Time to tell

Eating disorders are still misunderstood and mistaken. People see them as trivial and self-inflicted, instead of serious and life-threatening mental illnesses. 1.1 million people in the UK are affected, and 20% of those who become seriously ill can die prematurely. Young people aged 14 to 25 are most at risk.

90% of parents said they felt confident about discussing eating disorders with their children, but 45% of young people said they couldn't tell anyone about their problems

Someone with an eating disorder will often find it extremely difficult to tell anyone about their problem, even once they recognise it themselves, and this can lead to a dangerous delay in treatment.

Early treatment is crucial for recovery, and to avoid the long-term consequences to physical health and mental well-being.

We surveyed 1,000 young people with personal experience of an eating disorder, and asked them key questions about who they could tell; how long it took to seek help; and what change they would wish for in the world to make a difference to eating disorders.

Their answers were startling, and we were surprised by what we learned from them. We are committed to continuing this learning, and to keep listening to what they want to tell us. There has been too much secrecy and silence. It's time to tell.

Time to tell parents

A recent survey[1] asked parents about eating disorders and the answers they gave were very different from what the young people we spoke to told us.

90% of parents said they felt confident about discussing eating disorders with their children, but 45% of young people said they couldn't tell anyone about their problems.

40% of parents said they would recognise the early signs, but only 21% of young people said their parents had noticed the eating disorder first.

We want to make sure that parents have the information they need so that they can talk to their children if they are concerned. And young people need to feel confident that in telling their parents, they will be understood.

'I had continual arguments with my family that I was fine. I wasn't. I was dying.'
'My parents had a very hard time understanding what I was going through.'
'The change I would wish for is for parents to understand more about how they can help. My family didn't know how to deal with it.'

Time to tell the doctor

The sooner someone gets the help they need, the more likely they are to make a full recovery. Yet 62% of young people told us they waited more than six months before seeking help. This crucial delay could have given the eating disorder time to take hold of them, and for their treatment to take longer to be effective.

And then doctors themselves have said they need to be better at making early diagnoses[2].

We want to make sure that GP training on eating disorders is up-to-date, and gives them the skills to make diagnoses early, so that the road to recovery can begin as soon as possible.

'I couldn't find help when I needed it, and when I did I felt like a freak.'
'Why is it that when you have a broken leg, they know exactly what to do, but when you go for help with an eating disorder, they are flummoxed?'
'The change I would wish for is for doctors to treat you with the same compassion as if you had a physical illness.'

Time to tell the media

The media is playing an increasingly powerful role in all our lives. We are surrounded every day by ever more sophisticated ways of advertising and promotion of a skinny ideal. Eating disorders are not caused by the media – it's more complex than that – but young people had very strong views about the media's part and how it could help.

We asked if there was anything in the world that could help prevent eating disorders, and 42% said the media showing more 'real' bodies. This compared to parents understanding and doctors knowing more at 20% each.

It is time to tell the truth about eating disorders. They are a serious mental illness, with serious consequences if untreated. There are young people who are willing to tell their story like it is – and they are ready for it to be heard.

'Why can't the media promote healthy, normal-sized people?'

'It gives us the impression that thin is beautiful and that we have to be thin if we want happiness and success in life.'

'The change I would wish for is to stop praising thin celebrities and constantly printing articles about dieting over and over.'

Notes

1 BBDO TNS online panel survey December 2005.
2 Health of the Nation survey (November 2005) by Dr Foster for Norwich Union found 69% of GPs felt the NHS failed patients with eating disorders: www.healthofthenation.com/the_index4.htm.

The call to action

The Eating Disorders Association (EDA) calls on all political parties to make a commitment to listen and respond to these future electorates' views. Eating disorders are still too often misunderstood, misdiagnosed

and even left untreated – leaving young lives at risk and young potential wasted.

'The political door is now open for an intense educational programme on eating disorders. Mental health and food are high on the political agenda.'
Dr Ian Gibson, MP, Science and Technology Commons Select Committee, and chair/member of many all party health groups.

We asked if there was anything that could help prevent eating disorders, and 42% said the media showing more 'real' bodies

---

'It is important that people with eating disorders know where to turn for advice, feel able to ask for help, and receive constructive assistance when they seek it. This important research indicates that eating disorders sufferers frequently do not seek or receive the quality of treatment needed to overcome their conditions. I know from my own constituency experience the lack of specialised help and support.'
Professor Steve Webb, MP, Liberal Democrat Shadow Secretary of State for Health.

'Eating disorders are very often a manifestation of underlying emotional or behavioural problems. While anorexia can become recognisable as young people become progressively thinner, bulimia can go unrecognised for a long time. In either case, early intervention is important, yet far too often services

are not available, or are subject to a "postcode lottery" as affected one of my constituents. This research supports our call for increased priority for mental health services.'
Andrew Lansley, MP, Conservative Shadow Secretary of State for Health.

'What this report highlights is the need to help parents and GPs listen to both overt and covert aspects of an eating disorder. Research has proved that the earlier treatment and help is available the better the outcome.'
Professor Janet Treasure, King's College London, Chief Medical Advisor to EDA.

'In today's body- and image-conscious culture, where to be very thin is considered beautiful and to be at normal weight is unacceptable, dieting and eating disorders are increasingly common. Biology plays a cruel trick on young people in Britain's fat-phobic society. It is time to tell young people, parents, the medical profession and the media that patients with mental illnesses must be accorded the same respect and treatment as those presenting with physical problems.'
Dr Peter Rowan, eating disorders consultant at the Priory Hospital, Roehampton.

Report published 6 February 2006 by the Eating Disorders Association, 103 Prince of Wales Rd, Norwich, NR1 1DW. Tel 0870 770 3256, email info@edauk.com.

■ The above information is reprinted with kind permission from the Eating Disorders Association. Visit www.edauk.com for more information.
© Eating Disorders Association

Media victims

Should we blame the glossies for the growing problem of eating disorders in our society?

By Christina Stark

We are confronted on a daily basis with a barrage of images depicting and glamorising thin women. Because the media in general – and glossy magazines in particular – are seemingly obsessed by the idea that thin equals beautiful, it is easy to understand why the media have been directly blamed for causing eating disorders.

Most eating disorder experts contend that there is far more to an eating disorder than a simple desire to imitate images of emaciated models. But there's little doubt that the media is responsible for putting pressure on some women who already feel vulnerable. To support this idea, eating disorder counsellors cite the fact that women constantly say they feel inadequate because of their inability to lose weight and therefore look 'beautiful'.

Most eating-disorder experts contend that there is far more to an eating disorder than a simple desire to imitate images of emaciated models

Eating disorders are generally believed to be the result of unresolved psychological and emotional issues. The sufferer will normally discover that losing weight – either through extreme dieting or binge-eating followed by vomiting and/or the use of laxatives – establishes a form of control unavailable to the sufferer in any other area of their life. Once an eating disorder takes root, body image becomes distorted and the individual begins to feel she or he can never be thin enough.

One of the biggest problems with recovery from an eating disorder is that those in recovery remain obsessed by body size and shape. Treatment is often required to alleviate the 'horror' of becoming a healthy weight. Also, as recovery begins, the problems underlying the disorder often surface. These issues, which are varied and complex, might include fear of sexuality, fear of becoming an adult, responsibility and identity issues or loss and separation issues.

Many eating disorders occur almost accidentally when very young women begin to diet. Having achieved their dieting goal, they are encouraged by their peers and their own ability to control the process to take the diet further. They eventually become totally obsessed with dieting and food, until it dominates their life.

Perhaps the most important message to take away from the escalating problem of eating disorders is that, for all of our progress as women, we still don't feel comfortable and confident about our body image. It's interesting to note that the problem of eating disorders is also beginning to grow rapidly amongst males. This raises issues about the pressures and values inherent in our society.

For more information, contact the Eating Disorders Association:
- Adult helpline: 0845 634 1414 (10.30am-8.30pm Mon-Fri)
- Youth helpline: 0845 634 7650 (4.30pm-8.30pm, Mon-Fri)

■ The above information is reprinted with kind permission from iVillage UK. For information on this and other issues, please visit the iVillage UK website at www.iVillage. co.uk.

© iVillage UK

Body mass index by age and sex

Body mass index (BMI), by age and sex. Percentage of adults aged 16 and over with a valid height and weight measurement, 2004.[1]

Men

Age	20 or under	Over 20-25	Over 25-30	Over 30[2]
16-24	20.2%	48.8%	23.1%	7.9%
25-34	4.1%	37%	41%	17.9%
35-44	2.1%	22.4%	50.3%	25.2%
45-54	0.5%	21.7%	48.2%	29.6%
55-64	0.7%	21.7%	47.5%	30.1%
65-74	1.6%	22.2%	48.4%	27.8%
75+	2.5%	24.1%	54.4%	19%

Women

Age	20 or under	Over 20-25	Over 25-30	Over 30[2]
16-24	16.4%	47.4%	24.1%	12.1%
25-34	8.7%	43.2%	31.2%	16.9%
35-44	5.5%	40.1%	30.4%	24%
45-54	3.8%	33%	35.9%	27.3%
55-64	1.7%	29.3%	37%	32%
65-74	3.5%	27.9%	39.9%	28.7%
75+	3.8%	29.7%	45.9%	20.6%

1. Weighted for non-reponse.
2. Includes over 40.

Source: 2005, NHS Health and Social Care Information Centre. Crown copyright.

Helping a friend

Knowing what to do for the best can turn into a real burden when you're concerned about a friend's eating behaviour. Use our step-by-step guide and you'll provide the best support for your friend and yourself

Step one: approach with caution

If you suspect your friend has eating problems but are not sure, the worst thing you can do is to go in all guns blazing. Here are some dos and don'ts to help you get a conversation started.

Do:

- set a time to talk: make sure you will be alone and have plenty of uninterrupted time together;
- tell them your concerns: keep a caring tone and gently use specific examples that have worried you the most;

Demanding to know everything or offering over-simplified solutions such as 'Just start eating and you'll be fine,' are not helpful

---

- encourage them to talk: don't make it a lecture, listen to your friend's reactions and accept what they tell you without being judgemental.

Don't:

- force them to talk: if your friend isn't ready to discuss the problem, that's OK – if you try to force too much too soon it could push them away. At this stage the most important step is them understanding that you are concerned and you are there to support them;
- argue: you may not agree with your friend's reactions, especially if they deny that they have a problem, but arguing about it will only make the matter worse and run the risk of your trust being lost. Again, repeat the reasons for

your concern and make it clear that you are there if they need someone to talk to.

Step two: think about yourself

Helping a friend through an eating disorder is a tough ride for you as well and you may well find that in amongst all the worrying about another person you forget about your own needs. If your friend is hiding their problems and the burden of carrying the secret is too much for you, you may have to talk to a third party. Trying to play the hero by taking everything on yourself will leave you exhausted, and that's no good to someone who needs your support. As well as taking some of the strain off of you, telling someone else will give extra support to your friend in the long run.

Step three: keep communicating

- Be patient: demanding to know everything or offering over-simplified solutions such as 'Just start eating and you'll be fine,' are not helpful. Instead, offer continued support.
- Focus on the good: remind your friend of their good points and focus on personality rather than appearance. Low self-esteem is a common characteristic of people with eating disorders, so let them know why they are so special. Avoid blaming them or making them feel guilty: use the word 'I' instead of 'you'.
- Don't skirt around the subject: talk openly about your worries. If you avoid it, so will they.

Step four: act by example

- Be a role model: continue to eat a balanced diet and try to exercise regularly. Do this openly without making it a big issue.
- Swot up: learn as much you can about eating disorders through books, websites and organisations. Knowing the facts will help you if your friend tries to blind you with inaccurate information about their eating habits.

- The above information is reprinted with kind permission from TheSite.org. Visit www.thesite.org for more information.

© *TheSite.org*

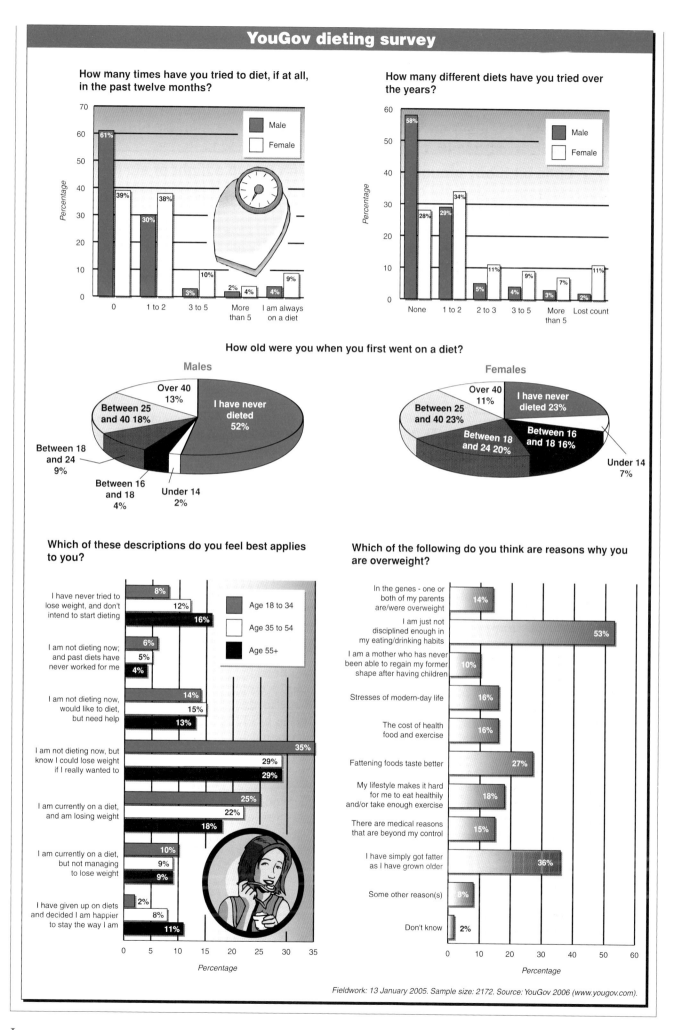

How many times have you tried to diet, if at all, in the past twelve months?

- Male
- Female

Percentage

	0	1 to 2	3 to 5	More than 5	I am always on a diet
Male	61%	30%	3%	2%	4%
Female	39%	38%	10%	4%	9%

How many different diets have you tried over the years?

- Male
- Female

Percentage

	None	1 to 2	2 to 3	3 to 5	More than 5	Lost count
Male	58%	29%	5%	4%	3%	2%
Female	28%	34%	11%	9%	7%	11%

How old were you when you first went on a diet?

Males

- Over 40 13%
- Between 25 and 40 18%
- Between 18 and 24 9%
- Between 16 and 18 4%
- Under 14 2%
- I have never dieted 52%

Females

- Over 40 11%
- Between 25 and 40 23%
- Between 18 and 24 20%
- Between 16 and 18 16%
- Under 14 7%
- I have never dieted 23%

Which of these descriptions do you feel best applies to you?

- Age 18 to 34
- Age 35 to 54
- Age 55+

	18-34	35-54	55+
I have never tried to lose weight, and don't intend to start dieting	8%	12%	16%
I am not dieting now; and past diets have never worked for me	6%	5%	4%
I am not dieting now, would like to diet, but need help	14%	15%	13%
I am not dieting now, but know I could lose weight if I really wanted to	35%	29%	29%
I am currently on a diet, and am losing weight	25%	22%	18%
I am currently on a diet, but not managing to lose weight	10%	9%	9%
I have given up on diets and decided I am happier to stay the way I am	2%	8%	11%

Percentage

Which of the following do you think are reasons why you are overweight?

	Percentage
In the genes - one or both of my parents are/were overweight	14%
I am just not disciplined enough in my eating/drinking habits	53%
I am a mother who has never been able to regain my former shape after having children	10%
Stresses of modern-day life	16%
The cost of health food and exercise	16%
Fattening foods taste better	27%
My lifestyle makes it hard for me to eat healthily and/or take enough exercise	18%
There are medical reasons that are beyond my control	15%
I have simply got fatter as I have grown older	36%
Some other reason(s)	8%
Don't know	2%

Percentage

Fieldwork: 13 January 2005. Sample size: 2172. Source: YouGov 2006 (www.yougov.com).

put the figure as high as 7%. The true costs are undoubtedly much greater, as not all obesity-related conditions are included in the calculations.

How does excess body fat impact health?

Overweight and obesity lead to adverse metabolic effects on blood pressure, cholesterol, triglycerides and insulin resistance. Some confusion of the consequences of obesity arise because researchers have used different BMI cut-offs, and because the presence of many medical conditions involved in the development of obesity may confuse the effects of obesity itself.

The non-fatal but debilitating health problems associated with obesity include respiratory difficulties, chronic musculoskeletal problems, skin problems and infertility. The more life-threatening problems fall into four main areas: cardio-vascular problems; conditions associated with insulin resistance such as type-2 diabetes; certain types of cancers, especially the hormonally related and large-bowel cancers; and gallbladder disease.

The likelihood of developing type-2 diabetes and hypertension rises steeply with increasing body fatness. Confined to older adults for most of the 20th century, this disease now affects obese children even before puberty. Approximately 85% of people with diabetes are type-2, and of these, 90% are obese or overweight. And this is increasingly becoming a developing world problem. In 1995, the emerging market economies had the highest number of diabetics. If current trends continue, India and the Middle-Eastern crescent will have taken over by 2025. Large increases would also be observed in China, Latin America and the Caribbean, and the rest of Asia.

Raised BMI also increases the risks of cancer of the breast, colon, prostrate, endometrium, kidney and gallbladder. Chronic overweight and obesity contribute significantly to osteoarthritis, a major cause of disability in adults. Although obesity should be considered a disease in its own right, it is also one of the key risk factors for other chronic diseases together with smoking, high blood pressure and high blood cholesterol. In the analyses carried out for *World Health Report 2002*, approximately 58% of diabetes and 21% of ischaemic heart disease and 8 to 42% of certain cancers globally were attributable to a BMI above $21kg/m^2$.

What can we do about it?

Effective weight management for individuals and groups at risk of developing obesity involves a range of long-term strategies. These include prevention, weight maintenance, management of co-morbidities and weight loss. They should be part of an integrated, multi-sectoral, population-based approach, which includes environmental support for healthy diets and regular physical activity. Key elements include:

- creating supportive population-based environments through public policies that promote the availability and accessibility of a variety of low-fat, high-fibre foods, and that provide opportunities for physical activity.
- promoting healthy behaviours to encourage, motivate and enable individuals to lose weight by eating more fruit and vegetables, as well as nuts and whole grains;
- engaging in daily moderate physical activity for at least 30 minutes;
- cutting the amount of fatty, sugary foods in the diet;
- moving from saturated animal-based fats to unsaturated vegetable-oil based fats;
- mounting a clinical response to the existing burden of obesity and associated conditions through clinical programmes and staff training to ensure effective support for those affected to lose weight or avoid further weight gain.

- The above information is reprinted with kind permission from the World Health Organization. Please visit www.who.int for more information.

© World Health Organization

Obesity in Europe

Information from the World Health Organization

Overweight (body mass index [BMI] over 25) affects some 25 to 75% of the adult population in the WHO European region. Indeed, the average BMI for the region is nearly 26.5.

Obesity (BMI over 30) affects up to one-third of the adult population in the European region. It is estimated that almost 400 million adults in the region are overweight and about 130 million are obese.

Childhood obesity is an acute health crisis. Various studies estimate that 10 to 30% of European children aged seven to 11 years and 8 to 25% of adolescents (14 to 17 years) carry excess body fat.

Rapid increase

If prevalence continues to increase at the same rate as in the 1990s, it is estimated that about 150 million adults in the region will be obese by 2010. The figures show a clear upward trend, even in countries with traditionally low rates of overweight and obesity such as France, the Netherlands and Norway. The gap between the western and eastern parts of the region is closing rapidly.

Growing economic costs

Obesity creates a major economic burden through loss of productivity and income, and consumes some 2 to 8% of overall health care budgets. Spain, for example, recently reported that nearly 7% of health care costs were directly or indirectly associated with obesity. In the eastern half of the region, this figure is up to 5%.

- The above information is reprinted with kind permission from the World Health Organization. Visit www.who.int for more information.

© World Health Organization

Obesity and genetics

Genetic discovery offers hope of treatments for obesity

By James Randerson, Science Correspondent

Scientists have discovered the first common genetic mutation to be linked to excessive weight, which they hope will lead to treatments to tackle obesity. People whose genetic make-up includes two copies of the mutation are on average 22% more likely to be obese. But the research suggests the double mutation increases obesity risk in African-Caribbean people by 136%.

More than one-fifth of UK adults are obese and a further half of men and one-third of women are classified as overweight. Obesity is a risk factor for heart disease, diabetes and premature death and last month, the US Surgeon General, Richard Carmona, warned that the health consequences of America's obesity epidemic would dwarf the threat from terrorism.

> *More than one-fifth of UK adults are obese and a further half of men and one-third of women are classified as overweight*

In the study, Alan Herbert at Boston University Medical School and his team looked at more than 100,000 common genetic mutations in nearly 700 American volunteers. One mutation – named rs7566605 – made carriers more likely to be obese when presenting as a double copy. To confirm the association was more than chance, they looked at five other study populations – including European children and African-American adults. Four of the five gave the same result and the increased risk conferred by the gene was much higher in the African-American group, the team reports in *Science*.

'When you do it in independent populations around the world using independent laboratories and come up with same answer it is a very powerful reason to believe it is true,' Professor Herbert said. Other rare mutations that cause extreme obesity have been identified, but this is the first mutation that influences obesity in the general population. He stressed that there were probably several other common mutations involved in obesity and that diet and exercise were also important.

'It's not 100% determinative that if you have the gene you get obese. People often ask me what I would do if I had the mutation. If I could control my weight by diet and exercise then I wouldn't worry.'

Beckie Lang at the UK's Association for the Study of Obesity agrees. 'Whatever underlying genes we have, what we do on top of those is more significant. Therefore it is crucial that we follow healthy eating patterns and an active lifestyle to prevent weight gain and other ill-health.'

Professor Herbert's team is not sure yet what the mutation does, but it is just upstream on the DNA from a gene involved in making fat, so they believe it is probably involved in controlling that gene. The team

> *Scientists have discovered the first common genetic mutation to be linked to excessive weight, which they hope will lead to treatments to tackle obesity*

thought it changed the level of the gene or the way that it is made. 'You could imagine that the whole fat pathway could be amplified and turned into hyperdrive.'

Other researchers said the discovery offers hope for treating obesity by controlling the gene, for example with drugs.

14 April 2006

Children's fruit and vegetable consumption

Children's fruit and vegetable consumption, by survey year and sex. Children aged 5 to 15, 2001-2004; portions per day.

1. Weighted for non-response.   Source: 2005, NHS Health and Social Care Information Centre. Crown copyright.

Measuring child obesity

Childhood obesity measurements in schools could do more harm than good, warn researchers

The government's recently announced initiative to screen the weight of four and 10-year-olds in schools could be psychologically harmful to children and even result in some developing eating disorders, warn researchers from Loughborough University.

Supporters say the tests, which will measure the children's Body Mass Index (BMI), will help to increase parental awareness of obesity, while opponents claim the initiative could lead to overweight children being misinformed about the state of their health and, even worse, being bullied.

The Loughborough researchers – Dr Emma Rich, Professor John Evans and Rachel Allwood, from the School of Sport and Exercise Sciences – agree that the potentially damaging effect on the children themselves could outweigh the benefits.

They have also expressed concerns over the use of BMI as a measuring tool, as research evidence suggests it to be very imprecise, and not a method that should be used on its own or casually to make judgements about a person's 'health'.

The team's opinions stem from their research into the experiences at school of girls and young women suffering from eating disorders, such as anorexia nervosa and bulimia. Their findings revealed that many sufferers strongly believe that their illness was nurtured or exacerbated, or sometimes even caused, albeit inadvertently, by the well-meaning actions of teachers and health experts in schools.

'Our research indicated that schools are increasingly pressing children to monitor their own diets, body shapes and levels of physical activity, which can unintentionally cause children to become anxious about their appearance, their weight and the food they're eating, when they have no need to be,' says Dr Rich.

Some of the young women interviewed as part of the team's study recalled traumatic experiences of being weighed in schools, which led to them becoming increasingly unhappy with their bodies. One girl commented: 'I used to be overweight, and I remember one time at school when the whole class got weighed. The teacher said, "Oh, it's the big one" and I was the heaviest in the year.'

Dr Rich continues: 'The pressures on children to monitor their bodies are relentless, and they're not just confined to school in PE and health lessons, they occur everywhere – in playgrounds, at lunchtimes, in corridors, on TV and websites, and in the home.

'The pressures on children to monitor their bodies are relentless'

'It's therefore unsurprising that recent surveys have shown that many young people who believe they are overweight or obese definitely are not.'

Based on their own and others' research evidence, the Loughborough team believe that a degree of panic has been generated about the issue of obesity, and child obesity in particular, which is often ill-founded. Children are increasingly considered to be an 'at-risk' group. As a result, governments around the world are investing a great deal of money in a range of new school-based health imperatives that focus on getting young people to exercise more, change their diets and lose weight.

'The initiatives being proposed to tackle the issue are driven by an assumed connection between claims of escalating rates of obesity and particular lifestyle practices, such as a decline in physical activity, poor diet and too much time spent at a computer or watching TV. Many of these claims are patently false. It's now acknowledged by some researchers that the relationships between weight, diet, physical activity and health are far more complex and uncertain than is currently being suggested,' comments Dr Rich.

'While there may be health risks for individuals at the extreme ends of the weight continuum, for example those who are extremely thin or morbidly obese, there's a great deal we don't know about the relationship between weight, health and physical activity. Some studies suggest that people who are 'overweight' according to their BMI but are physically active, may well be healthier than their thinner counterparts who are not physically active. In other words, size, shape and weight might not be the issue at all.'

As well as the BMI measurements being introduced in the UK, other practices now in operation elsewhere include lunchbox inspections and health report cards, and it has been reported that in Australia schools have 'fat laps', where children considered to be overweight are required to run around the school field during lunchbreaks.

The Loughborough researchers say it is difficult to see how such degrading practices can be considered as positive. 'Such initiatives would be considered unethical and unjust in other social contexts. They could have a hugely negative impact on young people.

'If translated into policy and practice in schools, this latest measure will certainly damage the health of some children,' they warn.
20 June 2006

■ The above information is reprinted with kind permission from Loughborough University. Visit www.lboro.ac.uk for more information.
© *Loughborough University*

A quarter of youngsters are now obese

By Jenny Hope, Medical Correspondent

More than one in four children aged between two and 10 is overweight or obese, a report says.

If the trend continues, the overall cost of obesity could hit almost £5 billion by 2010, the report warns.

These children face a lifetime of weight-related health problems.

And their generation could be the first in decades to die at a younger age than their parents, on average.

Government watchdogs say Labour is in danger of missing its target to halt childhood obesity by the end of the decade.

They blame a lack of national and regional leadership for the failure to improve youngsters' diet and activity levels.

The report from the National Audit Office, the Healthcare Commission and the Audit Commission says slow progress is being made towards delivering on the target set for England in July 2004.

Audit Commission Chief Executive Steve Bundred said recent figures showed obesity had increased from 9.6 per cent of youngsters in 1995 to 13.7 per cent in 2003.

The proportion of children who were overweight or obese rose from 22.7 per cent to 27.7 per cent.

The cost of childhood and adult obesity to the health service is around £1 billion. There is a further £2.3 billion to £2.6 billion cost to the economy as a whole – this includes lost productivity. But Mr Bundred said the cost to the economy alone could rise to £3.6 billion by 2010, with more than £1 billion in costs to the NHS – a bill close to £5 billion.

He said: 'If the trend continues, this generation of children will be the first for many decades that doesn't live for as long as their parents.'

The report said there has been a lack of coordinated effort across three government departments.

The obesity target is the responsibility of the Department of Health, Department for Education and Skills and the Department for Culture, Media and Sport.

The report warned that a 'lack of timely guidance' had made organisations unclear about their roles.

As a result, those further down the delivery chain may be wasting resources on interventions that fail to target at-risk children.

The report's recommendations include the need for better local guidance on initiatives, such as increasing use of school sports facilities outside school hours.

Public Health Minister Caroline Flint said childhood obesity was a priority for the government, and she recognised that 'we need to do more' to reach targets.

■ This article first appeared in the *Daily Mail*, 28 February 2006.

Children misclassified as obese

By James Meikle, Health Correspondent

One in eight children may be misclassified as overweight or obese, researchers say. But one in eight considered to have a normal body mass may have fat levels that could put them at increased risk of disease later in life.

A two-year study of almost 2,000 children aged between five and 18 has suggested that up to a quarter are misclassified by present checks.

The use of more sophisticated measurements using equipment costing £2,000 a time has shown that girls naturally carry proportionately 60% more fat than boys after puberty as their bodies prepare for childbearing.

By the age of 18, 24.8% of young women's bodies is made up of fat, compared with 15.4% in boys, who have more muscle and lean tissue.

However the overall picture that more than 30% of children in England, slightly more of them girls, are overweight or obese, remains unchanged.

The more sophisticated measurement, distinguishing between fat and muscle, could bring about significant differences in how individuals are treated. The equipment measures fat and non-fat composition by sending a small electric signal through the body via footplates and electrodes.

Andrew Prentice, from the London School of Hygiene and Tropical Medicine, said current methods based on looking at weight related to height and calculating body mass index 'has been helpful in raising awareness of the obesity epidemic'. But looking at the fat content was a better predictor of conditions such as high blood pressure, heart disease and diabetes.

6 September 2005

Hormone raises hope of victory in war on obesity

By Alok Jha, Science Correspondent

- *Rats' intake of food cut by half in research tests*
- *Questions still remain, warns specialist*

Scientists have discovered a hormone that suppresses appetite, raising hopes of new treatments in the fight against obesity, according to a study published today.

The hormone, named obestatin, halved food intake in rats and resulted in the animals losing one-fifth of their body weight.

Neville Rigby, Director of Policy at the International Obesity Taskforce, welcomed the discovery as another example of the fact that there was more to obesity than most people think. 'It helps to understand that it isn't simply, as people would have it, a question of obesity being a problem of sloth or gluttony. There are clearly mechanisms at work in the body which differentiate why one person becomes obese while another person seems to be unaffected. As we understand more of the science of obesity, we have more sympathy for the people affected.'

Anyone with a body mass index of greater than 30 is classed as obese, and the World Health Organization estimates there are some 300 million such adults worldwide. In the UK, more than one-fifth of the adult population is obese and a further half of men and one-third of women are classified as overweight. Obesity is a major risk factor linked to heart disease, diabetes and premature death.

Finding ways to combat this obesity epidemic has been a priority for many health researchers. Part of the work revolves around understanding the hormones that regulate body weight and food intake.

'This new research is a new piece of the puzzle in the complex system of bodyweight regulation,' said Katrina Kelner, Deputy Editor of life sciences at *Science*, where the study is published today.

'We knew before that a hormone called ghrelin that was produced in the gut and then secreted into the bloodstream, stimulates eating. The new work shows us that a new hormone, aptly called obestatin, is encoded by the same gene but exerts opposing effects – it inhibits food intake. This is a completely unexpected finding and it's really extraordinary to think the hormone had been sitting there in plain sight until these authors discovered it.'

> *Anyone with a BMI of greater than 30 is classed as obese, and the World Health Organization estimates there are some 300 million such adults worldwide*

Aaron Hsueh of the Stanford University School of Medicine, who led the team that made the obestatin discovery, said the work came out of a larger project to understand the role of hormones in human physiology.

He had been using the results of the human genome project to create a database of hormone receptors for which there were no known partner hormones. He then identified the ones that seemed most important biologically – the ones that have been conserved through evolution across many species.

The hunt led him to the gene that makes ghrelin, where he found DNA instructions for an unexpected hormone tacked on to the end.

Professor Hsueh set out to make the hormone, which he later named obestatin. 'We purified this hormone in rats' stomachs and tested its biological activity,' he said. 'To our surprise, we found that treatment with

obestatin actually suppresses food intake. The food intake [dropped] by more than 50%. Bodyweight is more like 20% down. So the same gene codes for two hormones and these two hormones have opposing actions in bodyweight regulation.'

Professor Hsueh said his discovery had lots of potential uses. 'Obestatin itself could have potential as an appetite-suppressing drug because one can use this small peptide by injection,' he said. 'The identification of the receptor for obestatin can also allow us to screen for new drugs that can also suppress appetite.'

Scientists have discovered a hormone that suppresses appetite, raising hopes of new treatments in the fight against obesity

---

He added, however, that people with obesity should not expect drugs too soon. 'Whether it's going to be effective or not it's too early to say,' he said.

Obesity researchers have been here before with another hormone – leptin – which signals to the brain to stop eating. In 1995 scientists discovered that, in mice, leptin had a near-miraculous effect of reducing bodyweight by nearly one-third. For a while it was hailed as a precursor to a wonder drug. But it never lived up to its promise in humans.

Matthias Tschöp, an obesity specialist at the University of Cincinnati, said there were several unanswered questions on obestatin. 'We don't know if obestatin administration to rats or mice causes some sort of illness or nausea, leading to a decrease in food intake,' he said.

And the hormone might have properties which are yet to be discovered. 'It could be that obestatin has a major effect on food intake but, at the same time, does something to energy expenditure that, at the end, balances things out,' Professor Tschöp said.

Many hormones are known to affect eating patterns inadvertently:

rexin, for example, makes people feel more aware of their surroundings and, as a result, eat more.

'It demonstrates nicely how a hormone that also influences food intake also has other biological functions and, at the end of the day, also influence food intake or bodyweight,' Professor Tschöp said. 'It could be that Mother Nature just put [obestatin] in place to regulate appetite or something whose primary function is something else.'

Mr Rigby cautioned against thinking that obestatin was the whole story. 'Each time we think we've found another of the key hormones, yet one more comes along,' he said. 'The more you know, the more there is to know. It's a big hill to climb in terms of accumulating all the knowledge we need to address obesity from the biological perspective.'

Notes

Hormone
Chemical messenger of the body. Hormones feed the brain information on the state of the body and allow the brain to respond. Ghrelin instructs the body to eat, while leptin and obestatin tell the brain that a person is full.

Body mass index
Common measure of a person's weight relative to their height. Above 25 is overweight; above 30 is obese.

Human genome project
Mapping project started in the late 1990s and completed in 2001: it sequenced human DNA and identified the location of the 30,000 genes which code for all the proteins needed for human life.

Hormone receptors
The proteins on cells that respond to the actions of specific hormones. Each hormone has its own type of receptor in the location where it is supposed to work.

Small peptide
A short strand of protein, the make-up of many hormones. Promising in terms of treatments because they are easy to make and deliver to patients.
11 November 2005
© *Guardian Newspapers Limited 2006*

Young people and five-a-day

Percentage of children eating the recommended five or more portions of fruit and vegetables per day, by age and sex. Children aged 5 to 15, 2004[1]

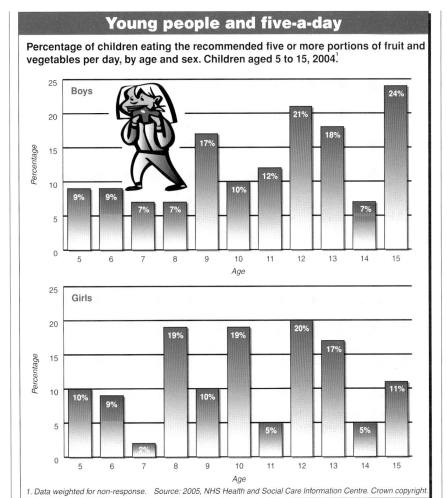

1. Data weighted for non-response.   Source: 2005, NHS Health and Social Care Information Centre. Crown copyright.

KEY FACTS

- Girls and women are 10 times more likely than boys and men to suffer from anorexia or bulimia. However, eating disorders do seem to be getting more common in boys and men. (page 1)

- An eating disorder can continue even when the original stress or reason for it has passed. Once your stomach has shrunk, it can feel uncomfortable and frightening to eat. (page 3)

- Anorexics who continue to starve themselves cause chemical and hormonal changes in their bodies that lead to loss of appetite, periods stopping, and feelings of depression and sadness. (page 4)

- Some of the psychological illnesses that can be (but are not always) found in people suffering with anorexia, bulimia and compulsive overeating are: obsessive compulsive disorder, depression, post traumatic stress disorder, bipolar and bipolar II disorder, borderline personality disorder, panic disorders and anxiety, dissociative disorder and multiple personality disorder. (page 9)

- The eating disorders anorexia and bulimia may be biological diseases rather than mental conditions, experts have said. Research suggests they are linked to infections which disrupt the body's immune system, causing it to attack the chemicals in the brain controlling appetite. (page 12)

- Over 85% of reported cases of bulimia occur in girls in their late teens and early twenties. Approximately 10% of people with the condition are men. (page 13)

- There is no one cause for binge eating, but like most eating disorders, it is generally seen as a way of coping with feelings of unhappiness, depression and low self-esteem. (page 15)

- It is estimated that as many as 1.15 million people in Britain suffer with an eating problem. Approximately 90,000 people are thought to be receiving treatment for either anorexia or bulimia. (page 20)

- Self-esteem is the way we feel about ourselves. Self-esteem means valuing your own worth and importance. (page 24)

- 90% of parents said they felt confident about discussing eating disorders with their children, but 45% of young people said they couldn't tell anyone about their problems. (page 25)

- 40% of parents said they would recognise the early signs of an eating disorder, but only 21% of young people said their parents had noticed the eating disorder first. (page 25)

- A survey asked young people if there was anything in the world that could help prevent eating disorders, and 42% said the media showing more 'real' bodies. This compared to parents understanding and doctors knowing more at 20% each. (page 26)

- Most eating disorder experts contend that there is far more to an eating disorder than a simple desire to imitate images of emaciated models. But there's little doubt that the media is responsible for putting pressure on some women who already feel vulnerable. (page 27)

- Despite the mistaken view that eating disorders are simply 'a slimmer's disease' they are recognised as serious health problems that need specialist care to help you deal with both the underlying psychological difficulties and the physical consequences. (page 28)

- Women are actually slimmer than they think according to new Deakin University research. But men consider themselves to be more muscular than they really are. (page 29)

- Although many people blame genetics, metabolism, hormones, or their glands for being overweight, these are in fact very rare reasons for weight gain. It's a simple equation: if you take in more energy (joules/calories) from food and drink than you use up, the body stores the excess as fat. (page 32)

- Globally, there are more than 1 billion overweight adults, at least 300 million of them obese. (page 33)

- Obesity and overweight pose a major risk for chronic diseases, including type 2 diabetes, cardiovascular disease, hypertension and stroke, and certain forms of cancer. (page 33)

- Childhood obesity is an acute health crisis. Various studies estimate that 10-30% of European children aged 7 to 11 years and 8-25% of adolescents (14 to 17 years) carry excess body fat. (page 34)

- Scientists have discovered the first common genetic mutation to be linked to excessive weight, which they hope will lead to treatments to tackle obesity. (page 35)

- One in eight children may be misclassified as overweight or obese, researchers say. But one in eight considered to have a normal body mass may have fat levels that could put them at increased risk of disease later in life. (page 37)

GLOSSARY

Anorexia nervosa
People with anorexia nervosa avoid eating and lose a lot of weight. These people often feel very fat, even when they are not. Without proper help, anorexia sufferers may become very weak and even die. It is most likely to occur in girls and young women, although prevalence among boys and men is increasing.

Bigorexia
Observed to be the 'opposite of anorexia', in which the sufferer is constantly worried they are too small. Found typically in body-building circles. There is no clinical guideline for this disorder, so it will not be diagnosed by a physician.

Binge eating disorder
Like bulimia nervosa, binge eating disorder involves dieting and bingeing, but not purging. It is distressing, but less harmful than bulimia. Sufferers are more likely to become overweight.

Body dismorphic disorder
A preoccupation or obsession with a defect in visual appearance, whether that be an actual slight imperfection or an imagined one.

Body mass index (BMI)
A simple formula that takes into account your weight and height. If you are a healthy weight, your BMI should be between 20 and 25. If it is over 25, you are likely to be overweight. People with a BMI of more than 30 are defined as being obese.

'Bulimarexia'
The symptoms of anorexia and bulimia are often mixed – some sufferers with symptoms of both diseases use this term to describe their condition.

Bulimia nervosa
Bulimia nervosa is characterised by binge eating, often of high-carbohydrate foods, and then 'purging' (making oneself sick) to get rid of the food. Bulimia sufferers may also use laxatives. It is most likely to occur in girls and young women, although prevalence among boys and men is increasing.

Compulsive eating
When people eat much more than their bodies need over a long period, or use food to comfort or distract themselves.

Eating disorder
An illness characterised by abnormal, dangerous eating habits. The most common eating disorders are anorexia nervosa, bulimia nervosa and binge eating disorder.

Night eating syndrome
Sufferers will put off eating until late in the day, then binge on food in the evenings. They will experience problems falling asleep and/or staying asleep.

Obesity
Someone with a body mass index (BMI) of over 30 is defined as being obese, meaning they are dangerously overweight. Such people should consider making serious changes to their diet and exercise habits. In the UK at the moment, around 17% of men and 21% of women are clinically obese and there is concern that the number of obese people, particularly children, is rising.

Orthorexia nervosa
An obsession with a 'pure' diet which interferes with a person's life. It becomes a way of life filled with chronic concern for the quality of food being consumed. There is no clinical guideline for this disorder, so it will not be diagnosed by a physician.

Pica
Defined as a compulsive craving for eating, chewing or licking non-food items or food containing no nutrition, e.g. chalk, plaster, ice. It is fairly common in pregnant women and symptoms usually disappear after the birth of the child.

Prader-Willi syndrome
A condition present at birth, believed to be caused by an abnormality in the genes. The sufferer has an insatiable appetite, caused by a defect in the hypothalamus – a part of the brain that regulates hunger – that causes the person to never actually feel full.

Puberty
From the Latin word 'pubertas', meaning grown-up or adult. It's the word given to all of the changes you go through from a child to an adult. This is a time when some young people may become affected by serious eating problems.

Serotonin
Serotonin is a neurotransmitter, a group of chemical messengers, that carry out communication in the brain and body. One of serotonin's roles is to mediate emotions and judgement. Recent research suggests serotonin is linked to the development of an eating disorder.

Sleep eating disorder
Sufferers tend to be overweight and have episodes of recurrent sleepwalking, during which time they binge on usually large quantities of food, often high in sugar or fat. Often, sufferers do not remember these episodes.

INDEX

ADDITIONAL RESOURCES

Other Issues *titles*

If you are interested in researching further the issues raised in *Eating Disorders*, you may want to read the following titles in the **Issues** series as they contain additional relevant articles:

- Vol. 125 *Understanding Depression* (ISBN 1 86168 364 2)

- Vol. 123 *Young People and Health* (ISBN 1 86168 362 6)

- Vol. 117 *Self-Esteem and Body Image* (ISBN 1 86168 350 2)

- Vol. 113 *Fitness and Health* (ISBN 1 86168 346 4)

- Vol. 100 *Stress and Anxiety* (ISBN 1 86168 314 6)

- Vol. 88 *Food and Nutrition* (ISBN 1 86168 289 1)

- Vol. 77 *Self-inflicted Violence* (ISBN 1 86168 266 2)

- Vol. 69 *The Media* (ISBN 1 86168 251 4)

- Vol. 19 *Looking at Vegetarianism* (ISBN 1 86168 191 7)

For more information about these titles, visit our website at www.independence.co.uk/publicationslist

Useful organisations

You may find the websites of the following organisations useful for further research:

- ANRED: www.anred.com

- ChildLine: www.childline.org.uk

- Deakin University: www.deakin.edu.au

- The Eating Disorders Association: www.edauk.com

- Institute of Psychiatry, King's College, London: www.iop.kcl.ac.uk

- iVillage UK: www.iVillage.co.uk

- Loughborough University: www.lboro.ac.uk

- NHS Direct: www.nhsdirect.nhs.uk

- The Royal College of Psychiatrists: www.rcpsych.ac.uk

- Something Fishy: www.something-fishy.org

- TheSite: www.thesite.org

- The World Health Organization: www.who.int

ACKNOWLEDGEMENTS

The publisher is grateful for permission to reproduce the following material.

While every care has been taken to trace and acknowledge copyright, the publisher tenders its apology for any accidental infringement or where copyright has proved untraceable. The publisher would be pleased to come to a suitable arrangement in any such case with the rightful owner.

Chapter One: Eating Disorders

Eating disorders, © Royal College of Psychiatrists, *Eating disorders: the risks*, © TheSite.org, *Can eating disorders cause permanent damage?*, © Institute of Psychiatry, King's College, London, *Genetics and biology*, © Something Fishy, *Are you at risk? Take a self-test*, © ANRED (Anorexia Nervosa and Related Eating Disorders, Inc.), *Associated mental health conditions and addictions*, © Something Fishy, *Reflections of my former self*, © Guardian Newspapers Ltd. 2006, *Anorexia could be physical, not mental*, © 2006 Associated Newspapers Ltd., *Bulimia*, © Crown copyright material is reproduced with the permission of the Controller of HMSO and Queen's Printer for Scotland, *Binge eating*, © Crown copyright material is reproduced with the permission of the Controller of HMSO and Queen's Printer for Scotland, *Other types of eating disorders*, © Something Fishy, *Eating problems*, © ChildLine, *What have eating disorders got to do with puberty?*, © Eating Disorders Association,

Time to tell, © Eating Disorders Association, *Media victims*, © iVillage UK, *Seeking treatment*, © Eating Disorders Association, *Study finds we are thinner than we think*, © Deakin University, *Helping a friend*, © TheSite.org, *YouGov dieting survey*, © YouGov.

Chapter Two: Obesity

Obesity, © TheSite.org, *Obesity and overweight*, © World Health Organization, *Obesity in Europe*, © World Health Organization, *Obesity and genetics*, © Guardian Newspapers Ltd., *A quarter of youngsters are now obese*, © 2006 Associated Newspapers Ltd., *Children misclassified as obese*, © Guardian Newspapers Ltd., *Hormone raises hope of victory in war against obesity*, © Guardian Newspapers Ltd., *Measuring child obesity*, © Loughborough University.

Photographs and illustrations:

Pages 1, 11, 17, 30: Don Hatcher; pages 5, 13: Bev Aisbett; pages 8, 15, 21, 32: Angelo Madrid; pages 9, 16, 26, 38: Simon Kneebone.

Craig Donnellan
Cambridge
September, 2006